GET CONNECTED

Tor Eneroth, Pleuntje van Meer, Niran Jiang, Phil Clothier and Hector Infer

ISBN: 978-1-4834-0141-6 (sc)
ISBN: 978-1-4834-0142-3 (e)

Lulu Publishing Services rev. date: 8/23/2013

Graphic design	Nona Bunea
Illustrations	Gerdur Ragnarsdottir
	Jan Eneroth
	Thomas Olsson
Editor	Fran Hamilton, Autumn St. John
Reproduction and print	Fototext AB
Copyright©	Tor Eneroth
	Pleuntje van Meer
	Niran Jiang
	Phil Clothier
	Hector Infer

April 2013

CONTENT

If you want a harvest in a year, grow a crop...
If you want a harvest in ten years, grow a tree...
If you want a harvest that will last for a life time, grow people.
-Chinese Proverb

Prologue

Industrialisation seeds humanity with greed and separation. Lost inside a dream of machines, we numb our senses by chasing tasks and activities. We sleep walk through our work with unexamined assumptions of growth and false sense of achievement. In pursuit of consumerism, we paralyse our human potential. Collegial connection is shredded by the rat race and competition. Under a structure of power and hierarchy, we march to our destruction through the very busy work we perform every day.

The crisis we face, both at a macro and micro level, is overwhelming in its scale and complexity. We could easily feel disempowered in our ability to challenge and act. Yet inside this very crisis is an impending transformation opportunity for humankind. Billions of years of universal intelligence is encoded in us since the beginning of time and space. Humanity is waking up to life's inherent potential to be and to become. People around the globe, young and old of all races, are taking actions to make the world a better place. Get Connected is a small initiative to support team development in the workplace, yet with a big ambition to tap into our human potential and aid collective evolution.

Get Connected is a collaborative effort among a group of highly experienced transformation facilitators, aiming to empower team leaders with a practical toolkit to help them build teams and grow team cultures. It is a do-it-yourself package to guide you through the framework, process and methodology of team development. It supports you to question the way you work, to examine the assumptions you behold and to build the connection you long for. The book is based on the belief that in most teams we have much more potential than we currently use, due to the way we organize and behave. It provides you with the possibilities to free more of that human potential by:

- Empowering you as a team leader, or team coach to connect your team members on a more subjective and emotional level.
- Helping you to see "the whole" journey in order to grow and create a more connected team, recognizing that it is not one or two events or workshops that make the difference, but rather the attention and respect you give your team by investing in time to connect and bond through dialogue around issues that are of individual and collective value to the team.
- Supporting you in planting and caring for something, in this case a group of human beings, that is continuously developing and growing, and inspiring you to take risks and go outside your own and your team's "safety zones", in order to explore and evolve together.

This book is not a mechanical manual to follow and live by, but an illustration of an organic process to live through. With a set of practical processes and tools, which we find most effective through our collective experiences for team development, we intend to provide you with a baseline plattform to experiment with and innovate from. It is a tool kit with words, not facilitation skills with senses. We ask you to play with it, trust your intuitive judgement, and discover what works or not through trial and error. Growing your team is an organic living process, which requires you to tap into the inner knowing of your team and to leverage group intelligence to co-create and co-evolve. We ask you to stay open to learn and strive to improve with humility.

Your personal development is a critical foundation for your success in growing your team and culture. Not only do you need to do the work with your team, but also you need to carry the work and be the change you wish to see. As a team leader, you are the role model and must walk the talk. How you treat your team members will set the ceiling for the level of bonding and depth of connections they experience with each other in the team. You need to challenge yourself to develop your own potential and evolve who you are as a leader.

Nature is the greatest teacher of our time, and offers generous antidotes to offset the imbalance accumulated since the Industrial Revolution. We use a simple tree metaphor throughout the book as a natural system symbol to guide our thinking. It illustrates a way of growth in nature to challenge institutional programming, balance intellectual models and stimulate human intuitive senses. Whenever feeling lost or struggling for ideas on your journey, we invite you to spend reflection time in nature to get recharged and inspired. Natural system thinking is a most effective and sustainable pathway for transformation.

We hope, through the good work you do in developing your people and growing your team, their innate human potential will reveal to make a difference in your organisation and our society. We envision deeply connected teams across organisations highly energised to achieve performance with greater learning, enjoyment and purpose. We imagine circles of connected human beings collaborating every day at work and radiating positive energy like ripples in the pond to make this world a better place for ourselves and our children.

1

INTRODUCTION

Recall a time when you were working in a team and had the feeling that everything was moving along just fine. The team was working well together; there was a sense of creativity and fun. You were producing great results. Remembering that time, ask yourself, 'What were the factors that made it all happen? How did it feel to work with the team?'

Take a few minutes and connect to that moment, and write down what made it happen? Who was involved? Describe it for yourself:

'Get Connected' has the ambition to recreate those special moments in teams and organisations that we all love to be part of. Times when you felt connected to the moment, the challenge, the task, the team and to yourself. It might have been a big challenge and at the same time was all understandable, meaningful and manageable. You felt connected! The goal of 'Get Connected' is to address the theory and the way of working to enable you to recreate the circumstances that resulted in such a successful and fulfilling work experience. Many leaders are waking up to the fact that the most important factor for the success of their team or organisation is culture (Culture = the values, beliefs and behaviours of a group). The way we behave together can make or break an organisation.

"We know we want to transform the culture but we don't know how!

This is a statement we are hearing from more and more leaders. Get Connected provides simple and practical steps to navigate what many people see as uncharted, complex and even dangerous territory. There is no doubt that this will take courage, commitment and a will to learn and grow. The good news is that others have managed to navigate this territory and report that the rewards far outweigh the costs. They even report that the journey brings new levels of fun, excitement, challenge and meaning to work. Are you ready for such an adventure at work?

In the closing years of the 20th Century, we did not know so much about the change process. When we entered this field some people thought that focus on values, vision and culture was a new age trend. It would come and go just as many other management theories and systems have done. Well it has not gone away; in fact the business world is waking up to the vital importance of this field of work for the good of all stakeholders and organisational success. Developing a culture is not like installing a machine. It is not static, but dynamic, something that is growing, very much like a garden. To grow a successful garden you must first prepare a good soil, plant the right seeds, and then maintain an environment which optimises the growth of healthy plants. For example ensure adequate water, sunlight and compost to stimulate strong growth and then also to root outthe weeds which impede the growth of the desired plants.

You then nurture your chosen plants through to maturity and harvest. 'Get Connected' will guide you in the selection of the effective leadership model and in staff engagement (preparing the soil); in instilling the desired values (the chosen seeds); and give you tips on how to carry out an ongoing dialogue in order to develop and mature your team in an optimal manner through to a successful roll-out (nurture through to harvest). Every culture is unique and it will grow differently depending on how you take care of it.

All gardeners and farmers know that manure is a great fertilizer so when issues and crises arise, you better be ready to work through them.

What is your vision for a connected and high performing team?

SCOPE & TARGET

The idea is that the leader (consultant or change agent) could use the 'Get Connected' concept and process (page 25-38) from start to finish. First, identify the desired vision, mission and values then instil and nurture them throughout the whole team or organisation. This work involves all stakeholders. You need to invest time to internalize and connect to each of these, which you do through dialogue workshops. Then you must make sure that the system and structure is aligned with the desired culture as measured and that you walk-the-talk. And last but not least you must take care of your culture by giving recognition to positive and wanted behaviour as well as acting firmly on unacceptable behaviour. In other words, this guide is not only about workshops and value statements. It is about daily operation that will help you develop your desired culture. This work is non-linear, to keep the flow of the book simple, we will describe it as more linear than we know it is.

You may be thinking that you are so busy that you can't afford to take time for developing your team and culture. Yes, this work does take time and commitment but you will soon discover the benefits in terms of improved relationships, productivity and outcomes far outweigh the time and effort.

How to use the book...

Some people will open this book and skim through looking for tools to help with specific issues or challenges in their team. Others will want the big picture and the deeper understanding that comes from the context and exploration of the topics in the early chapters. Both approaches are fine and yet ultimately your ability to facilitate transformation will be enhanced when the tools are used with the understanding that comes through deeper study and reflection. The most important thing that we learned about real transformation is that it cannot happen without dialogue. All these materials are designed to start new conversations and build understanding and trust.

If you only have time to do one thing, the most accessible tool in this book is called. "Important Questions" on page 69. This quickly connects you to your thoughts and feelings, your colleagues and allows you to create clarity and next steps for the big challenges facing you today.

THE BUSINESS CASE

Today CEOs and leaders are struggling with big questions such as:

- How to attract, motivate and keep talented people?
- How to increase profitability, sustainability and be present to the needs of all stakeholders?
- How to increase innovation, creativity, productivity, quality and customer satisfaction?
- How to increase accountability, openness and trust?
- How to run more engaging and productive meetings?
- How to handle the inevitable disagreements and conflicts?
- How to improve co-operation between virtual teams spread across different locations and countries?

Inevitably when a new group of people is formed to carry out a task, there is always a certain level of tension in the group. Questions like, 'Who are my new team members? Who is the leader? How can I contribute/be of value? Will I fit in?' These types of questions occupy a lot of the group's time and attention in the beginning. It is only after some time when these relationship issues have become clearer to the team members, that the group focuses more of its attention to the business task.

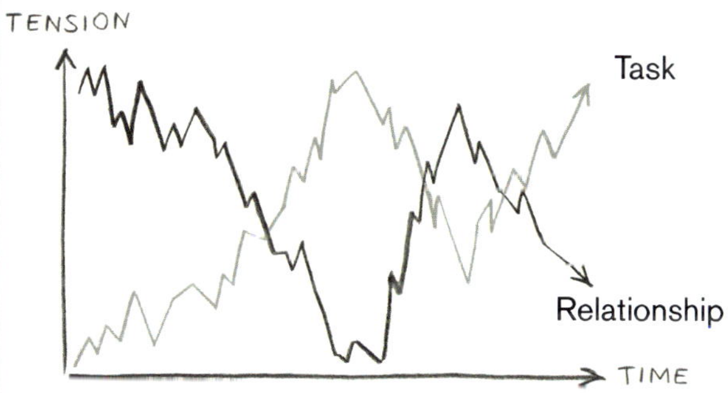

By investing in activities that clarify our relationship issues up front and throughout the team life cycle, we will enable the team to better focus on the task.

Our Attention

Working with the culture in our teams and regarding it as an investment will have clear pay-back for engagement and performance. As concluded by many leaders, this investment creates trust. Not only within the team but also with all the stakeholders connected to the organisation. Regarding trust, Stephen M. R. Covey states in a very simple and straight forward way how strong and clear the business case is in his book "Speed of Trust".

> Trust always affects two outcomes – speed and cost. When trust goes down, speed will go down and cost will go up. When trust goes up, speed will also go up and cost will go down. It's that simple, that real, and that predictable.

Investing time to connect the people to the team challenges, stakeholders and to themselves is vital for a successful performance. The importance of growing a shared culture and how this is a foundation for building trust and increasing productivity is also evident.

> Commitment is enhanced when all those involved share a common vision and values. Shared values build trust, and trust gives employees responsible freedom. Responsible freedom unlocks meaning and creativity. True power lies not in the ability to control but in the ability to trust. (Richard Barrett, 1998).

If you want more information on the business case for such a change, you can find some inspiring

What is your team level of trust, and how does it impact your team?

stories of change in real teams and organisations here. Including, "Cultural Capital - A fundamental driver of financial performance" www.valuescentre.com/resources

THE HUMAN PERSPECTIVE

"Research within organisations has for a long time emphasized strategic technological, financial and organizational aspects and marginalized the psychological, though it is the human motivation and creativity that create the results.
(Max Rapp Ricciardo, 2001).

It is easy to give all our attention to the rational and logical issues, like risk analysis, communication plans, gate structures, etc. because they are tangible and visible to everyone. These issues are also easy to structure, plan and follow up which in itself makes it easier for us to focus on them. However, even if it is not visible there is also an intangible and more subjective world that we have to learn to deal with. As human beings we have to recognize that we all have physical, emotional, mental and spiritual needs that we seek to fulfil. Based on thousands of culture surveys in recent years we can see clearly that the many cultures are focused strongly on the financial and efficiency/systems aspects of the organisation. But our personal values are more centred on making-a-difference and being part of something bigger than ourselves. There is also a high number of limiting values (e.g. blame, bureaucracy, hierarchy, exploitation, corruption) in the surveys that have a negative impact on the culture. These two issues create an unbalanced contract between the organisation and the people working in it. This in turn creates a stressful situation and in the long term could have an impact on both our physical and mental health. Without doubt, this will also have an impact on the business performance and outcomes.

While it is tempting to think that these issues can be addressed by stricter control and work processes, the truth is that these issues need to be addressed directly. That is done by proactively and systematically working with the culture and the intangible assets. If we do, we will not only free the full potential of our people in the team, we will also create a much more attractive and successful team or organisation. In order for each of us to take our whole self to work and free our full potential we must be given the opportunity to connect our own individual needs with the organisation needs. We can call this our "psychological contract" that we have with the team or organisation that we work in. If your personal needs overlap the organisation needs, you have a strong psychological contract. This will create higher meaning, energy, commitment and at the end better results.

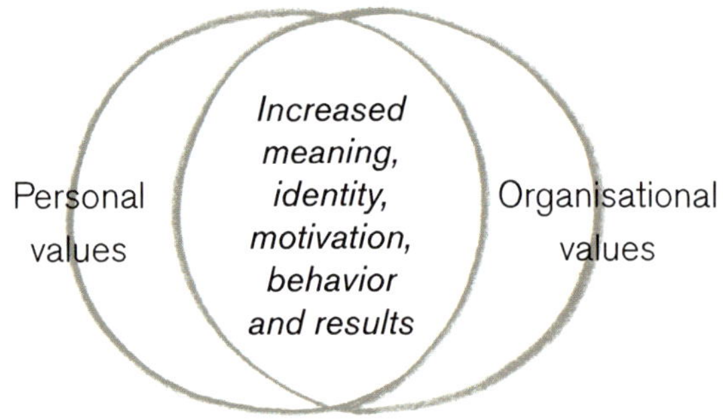

Another human perspective is health. It is important to build a healthy work environment that does not overstress our employees leading to burn-out. Having a strong psychological contract is one enabler for this. By applying the principles and tools presented in this guide you will create a healthier workplace from a mental and emotional perspective.

To what degree is the physical and psychological health of team members considered in daily operations and decision making? How does that impact your people and their ability to perform and grow?

COMMITMENT, KNOWLEDGE AND COURAGE

We have talked about the benefits of doing this work. It would be unfair not to mention that there are risks too. Many teams and organisations make a great start on this path with very good intentions. They go through the process of creating values and vision statements. This may create initial feelings of enthusiasm and hope for a better future but unless there is meaningful follow-through and action people quickly become disengaged and even cynical about the whole thing. We often tell leaders; "Unless you are committed to the long term process, please don't start. Doing half a job may even make things worse."

We often see impressive looking vision and values statements on the wall and people walk past them every day and ignore them because they see that the leaders are not walking the talk. This would be like getting enthusiastic about redecorating a room in your house. You go to the store and buy new wallpaper, paint and brushes but then leaving them stacked in the corner of the room that remains undecorated. The materials become a visible reminder of how dirty and messy and unloved the room really is.

If this has happened in your organisation, you may have heard your staff saying things like "We tried that teamwork and culture stuff and it didn't work." Let's take a moment to consider the reality and the most likely factors that may have led to failure.

If you have made a choice to change then you will need commitment, courage and knowledge in order to breakthrough and create the new way of being.

Lack of commitment

This work takes commitment and discipline. It takes time and energy and since every team and situation is unique, there are no single right answers to how the process will go or how quickly the benefits will start to emerge. There will undoubtedly be challenges and setbacks along the way but you need to have the commitment and tenacity to stay with it.

Lack of knowledge

Leaders and change agents may get stuck or may not even know how to start because they simply don't know how to facilitate the change. This book is designed to help get you started on the path but there are many other tools and resources available. If you get stuck you can always ask for help. Asking for external help may be the right answer. Asking your team members for help may be just what they were hoping for. Engaging the team in the design and execution of the change will create far greater engagement and the results will be far more beneficial. It takes courage to show vulnerability and ask for help. Leaders who are willing to admit they don't know often create new levels of respect and trust.

Lack of courage

It is said that organisations are perfectly designed to get the results they are getting. If you want new or better results then you need to have the courage to challenge the status quo and create something new. This means you have to have the courage to challenge the assumptions of the organisation, challenge each other and most importantly challenge your inner processes and your beliefs and behaviours. Organisational transformation starts with the personal transformation of the leaders.

Reflecting on past experience can often help us to achieve greater success in the future. Failure is often a more powerful teacher than success.

In your experience of previous efforts to improve team culture and performance, what were the factors that created success or failure?

THE STORY BEHIND THE BOOK

This book was originally published in 2009. It was masterminded by Tor Eneroth who at the time was the Culture Manager of Volvo IT and co-written with Per Hellsten and Sasha Hamilton. It was written to help Volvo project teams achieve new levels of connection, performance and delivery. The fact that the book is alive, well and still being distributed and used on a daily basis in Volvo IT a testament to its value and success.

In 2011 Tor joined Barrett Values Centre as the Network Director and this book has been updated and re-written for a wider audience of leaders, consultants and change agents in all types of organisations; teams, small businesses, corporations, NGOs, governments, schools and even citizen groups with common aims in mind.

Barrett Values Centre believes in realizing the human potential and provides powerful metrics that enable leaders to measure and to develop the cultures of their organizations, and the leadership development needs of their managers and leaders.

The core products of the organisation are the Cultural Transformation Tools (CTT). The Cultural Transformation Tools have been used to map the values of thousands of organisations and leaders in over 80 countries. The Cultural Transformation Tools are used by corporations, NGOs, government and municipal agencies, communities, schools and nations. The CTT values assessment instruments are available in over 50 languages.

What gets measured gets done.

Barrett Values Centre has developed a set of models and tools to measure the values and culture of teams, leaders and the whole organisation. The measurement includes factors such as the strengths that form positive foundations, the dysfunction beliefs and behaviours that undermine performance and the desired direction for the future. The Cultural Transformation Tools (CTT) provides leaders, consultants and coaches with one of the most detailed and comprehensive cultural diagnostics and values assessment instruments available.

CTT surveys provide the input you need to plan and manage your change initiatives, your cultural transformation programmes, your diversity interventions, your talent management and leadership development initiatives, and your customer feedback. They make the intangibles tangible and provide lead indicators for measuring individual and collective performance.

CTT is not the only method of measuring culture and it is vital that leaders choose the tools that will help them in bringing meaningful change. What makes CTT unique is that it does not start with a predefined structure of what 'good' looks like and it provides the vital link between individual, leadership and organisational development. The CTT assessments allow teams and large groups to create their own picture of their own unique desired culture and measure where they are in their journey by understanding their current culture.

You can find out more about the Cultural Transformation Tools and the underlying Barrett Seven Levels of Consciousness model here: www.valuescentre.com

After all, a book is just a book unless you do something with it. Through Get Connected we intend to help you transform your leadership capability, team and performance.

Barrett Values Centre has been certified users of their models and tools since 1998, and today there is almost 4000 CTT consultants and users around the whole world. The intention with this book is also to support and facilitate this global network of practitioners in their endeavors to create a values driven society. The book is a practical part of the CTT certification training today.

2

THE MINDSET

Throughout our whole life we shape and develop the way in which we look upon the world around us. Some call this 'mindset' or 'mental models', others call this 'stories' or 'dreams'. It is our fundamental beliefs and principles that govern the ways in which we think and act. Our mindset also impacts what we expect from others and what we are likely to impose on others to be "the right way". Our mindset defines our ability to understand and take on new thinking and it shapes the language we use to communicate. That is why it is so important for us to become more aware of our mindset and develop the language we use to interact with others. This section will explain some principles and beliefs that 'Get Connected' is based upon.

The following headings highlight some mindsets that we have found have a great impact on how we lead and take care of our culture in teams. We regard these as fundamental when creating a healthier and more productive culture. Please read these principles with an open and reflective mind – try to challenge your own current thinking in order to understand and appreciate new perspectives.

Every perspective is presented in a short and concise way followed by a self-reflecting question. Please take a few minutes to reflect and connect yourself with the question and your present mindset. Make your own notes in the space below each perspective of what comes to your mind.

THE TREE METAPHOR

An iceberg has only one ninth showing above the surface of the water, so eight ninths are actually invisible. The iceberg metaphor is often used to illustrate situations where there is a visible and tangible portion above the surface and a large, invisible and intangible portion below the surface. The tree has also a visible and an invisible part of it, and apart from an iceberg the tree is a living and growing system. We use the tree metaphor to illustrate the visible and invisible aspects of our lives. For each of us our reality consists of a part that is visible to others and also a part that is not. Often, the invisible side of life is a very large part of our individual perception of the reality.

If we use the tree metaphor to illustrate the reality of a corporation or a team, it could look like this; above the surface you have the rational and logical world. This world is looked upon as predictable and sequential. This part of our reality is usually expressed in plans, schedules, visions, goals, strategies, structures, processes, etc. It is usually based on the belief and mindset that everything can be controlled and predicted. Below the surface are the things you don't see but still exist, like our emotions and spirit. We usually talk about them as

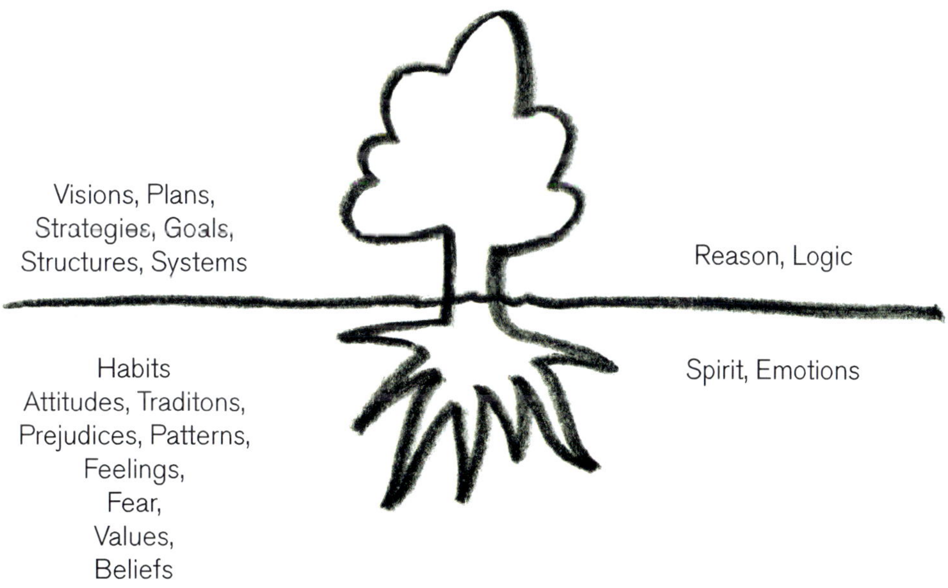

habits, traditions, attitudes, prejudices, patterns, feelings, beliefs, values, fears, etc. This part of our reality is something that we all know is there, but it is very difficult to predict and to manage. One could ask what is it that makes a tree grow strong and viable? The healthiness and strengths of the "roots" below the surface is a prerequisite for the "greenery" above the surface to flourish, grow flowers and fruits. You might say a tree needs to be well grounded in order to stand strong and grow during the change of seasons above the surface. It is the same with us human beings, we need to be well connected to our inner life in order to stand strong in both good and difficult times. The saying that "Culture beats Strategy – every time!", which in reality means that whatever logical strategy (above the surface) you may come up with, you will not succeed with it unless you align it to your current and desired culture (your attitude and emotions beneath the surface).

Reflective questions:

What do you pay most of your attention to – above or below the surface? Do you have a good balance?

TWO TYPES OF REALITY

Above the surface we focus very much on the reality related FORM and FUNCTION. In a project or team this is how we reach our targets on time, within budget, with the right resources and with the right quality. At the same time however, we must focus on the reality beneath the surface. If harnessed effectively in a team, the ENERGY and FLOW within us as human beings, will ensure a good working climate based on mutual respect, trust and a sense of belonging that gives us that all-important feeling of being of value and making a difference. Both realities motivate and stimulate us as human beings, but in different ways. Let us make one thing very clear though – neither of these two realities alone will result in a successful project or teamwork. You need to address both! Unfortunately there is a widespread tendency to believe that we will be successful if we focus enough and mainly on the rational issues like the FORM and FUNCTION. The real success formula is rather based on a balanced plan including both the objective and subjective reality of our work.

Reflective questions:

What makes up your reality? Is it based on Form and Function, on Energy and Flow, or both?

PEOPLE – AS OBJECTS OR SUBJECTS?

If we view our team members as objects, we would recognise their logical thinking and ability to perform tasks. So when selecting members of a team we would look at their records for how well they could contribute by using their HEAD and HANDS. While if we were to view our team members from a subjective perspective we would try to recognise what they value, their individual dreams and ambitions and what is important to them. What catches their HEART and SPIRIT? For any team member to be able to bring their whole self to work, they must be able to bring their HEART and SPIRIT as well as their HEAD and HANDS. In order to engage the full potential of every team member you need to recognize the importance of this balance.

Reflective questions:

What ignites your HEART and SPIRIT – and those of your team members? Are you/they aware of it and can you/they bring it to work?

USE OF "TIME"

A successful approach calls for an understanding and acceptance of the fact that the objective and subjective side of our reality are governed by two different types of time. The objective side above the surface is governed by the logical and sequential "chronological" or "clock" time, or as we illustrate it, TRIANGLE time. While the subjective side of below the surface is governed by "Kairos" time, which is time for the soul, time to connect or as we illustrate it, CIRCLE time. A group of people needs both, triangle time to define and set objectives and schedules and circle time to connect you and your team members to their attitudes, feelings, dreams etc. Circle time is also time to relax and heal, to get new energy and to get focused, while triangle time is needed to measure and follow up desired results and outcome.

Reflective questions:

What type of time do you work in mostly? Do you have enough time to connect (circle time)?

DISCUSSION VS. DIALOGUE

The word "discussion" comes from "desiccate", to break down into pieces, to define what is right and what is wrong, to state our opinion. We need discussions to determine and decide the rational side of our work. However, the word "dialogue" comes from building on each other's views and trying to identify underlying causes and learn from each other. There is great power in being able to clearly understand the distinction between dialogue and discussion and when to use which to get the most value out of a situation. We need to know whether a given situation needs discussion or dialogue, or both. Discussion is governed by the rational, logical triangle time, while dialogue is governed by the emotional and spiritual circle time which enables us to align, learn, understand and connect ourselves to the task we are to perform. We need to be clearly aware of this distinction, to be able to connect our rational reality with our emotional reality and thus utilise the full potential of team members.

Reflective questions:

How do you see the difference between discussion and dialogue – and do you know when and where to use each of them?

CHANGE VS. TRANSFORMATION

We set up teams and projects to develop, fix or reach something. In most cases it has to do with managing change. Change is what is happening around us. It could be new customer demands or increased competition, new techniques or a different organisation. Change happens in the environment around us and it takes place above the surface of our reality. In order for us human beings to take on change we need to adapt and align. This is called transformation. Transformation is what happens inside of us in order to move or develop our mindset and understanding or consciousness. Transformation is what is happening inside of us beneath the surface. So in order to manage projects and a team we need to recognise the need to deal with both the actual change and the human transformation. This is especially important to recognise when the change will have an impact on our identity, ego or beliefs.

Reflective questions:

How do you have a good balance between the need for the emotional transformation and the rational and logical change in your team?

INDIVIDUAL AND COLLECTIVE

To take on change and enable transformation, we need to recognise that our reality not only consists of both the objective and subjective perspectives, but that there also exists both a collective and individual reality. We need to recognise the fact that what is shared and understood by a group actually consists of the collective sum of individual consciousness and understanding by each person of that group. In order for your group to reach a defined objective and perform tasks in a co-ordinated, effective and efficient way you must invest in circle time. This enables each individual to connect themselves both to the objectives, tasks and to the values and principles that the team calls for before they can successfully complete it.

Reflective questions:

How do you make sure that each individual is connected to the objectives and tasks of your team?
How do you ensure that the individual and collective views are aligned?

A WHOLE HUMAN SYSTEM

If we put it all together it could be illustrated in four quadrants that make a Whole Human System. The tree metaphor would then illustrate our team as operating in a system with an environment that consists both of a rational/logical world and an emotional/spiritual world. The team output will be impacted by what is happening in the environment around and how we as individuals and as a collective group view and share our objective and subjective realities. In order for a team to reach its objectives we need to work and align each quadrant, because they are dependent on each other. And we need to realise that this is a whole system approach that calls for actions in all four dimensions at the same time.
See the illustration below.

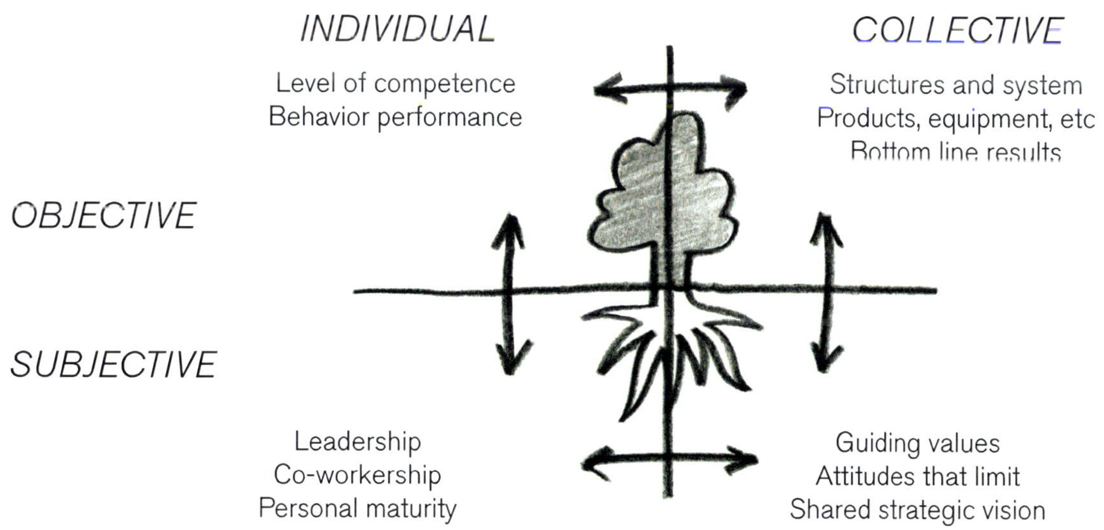

In the collective subjective dimension there are shared directions, collective dreams, i.e. our desired state. You must also make it possible for the individuals to align to their subjective side (both conscious and unconscious), internalize the change and see themselves in the future desired state before you can expect the team to change.

Reflective questions:

How do you work in all four quadrants? Do you tend to favour one or two? Why?

3

THE CONCEPT

We have chosen 'Get Connected' to name this mindset for culture in teams. This choice is based on the mindset that we are part of a whole human system in an environment that is interconnected. And that we need to create both understanding and awareness of how all these things relate to each other. It is about connecting to different worldviews. Connecting the tangible and the intangible; to connect yourself, to connect with each other and to connect to other key players. The challenge when connecting is to respect that we as human beings connect through talking, through dialogue and through reflecting.

A team that has connected through talking about their purpose, ambitions, and what they agree is important will also create a stronger identity, spirit and meaning.

'Get Connected' consists of five fundamental areas that you continually need to invest time in and connect to, in order to build the foundation for a solid, shared and successful team culture. Some teams need to focus more on only a few of these fundamental areas, while others may need to work with them all. This much depends on the development stage, participants and contextual needs. All areas are addressing different parts of our whole human system and are interlinked and dependent on each other. You need to find out where you have a shared and strong connection already, and where you should strengthen your connection.

These connections must also be regarded as something that is growing or changing over time, which means that you must not only address these issues at the forming stage of a team, yet rather to approach it as a continuous learning.

Please take the time to reflect on the questions on the following pages with your team to find out where you need to invest more time to connect.

The five fundamental areas to connect to are:

1. Our **REALITY**
2. **ME**
3. Our **AMBITIONS**
4. **US**
5. Our **LEARNING**

Connect to our **REALITY**... *the big picture!*

We need to create an understanding of how our team contributes to the development of the internal and external business environment, society and in the world in general. It is about appreciating a more extensive purpose and meaning of the team, putting the work that needs to be done into a greater context.

It is about creating a holistic view of the position that a team has and takes in the corporate universe. Understanding the customer challenges and how the team can create value for all its stakeholders. It is about getting an understanding of the Whole Human System that the team is part of.

Optional Tools:

1. Stakeholder Analysis .... p. 60
2. Connect to the Customer .... p. 62
3. Open Space .... p. 66
4. Important Questions .... p. 69

Questions to reflect upon could be:

1. *Who are the team's stakeholders and what specific dreams, expectations and demands do they have?*

2. *What contribution and value will the team add to its customers, partners and owners?*

3. *What environmental and/or societal impact will or can the team have in a long term perspective?*

Connect to ME... *my passion and values!*

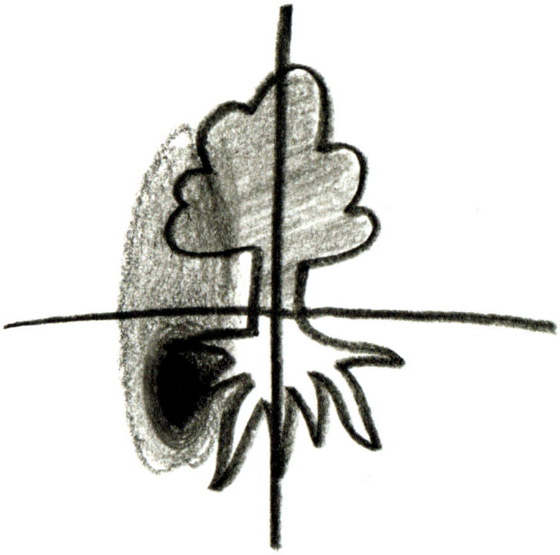

In this endeavor as a team, we have clear objectives: To understand who we are, what we believe in and strive for as individuals. And as individuals how we can connect and contribute to the whole system and bring our whole selves to work. To create a joint understanding of each other as individual team members by sharing who we are among the team members.

Optional Tools:

Questions to reflect upon could be:

1. What are your passions in life and what gives you energy?

2. Is who you are and what you stand for something you feel you can bring to this team?

3. Is what you find important being appreciated and recognised in this team?

4. What makes your "heart sing"? Does the team offer you this?

5. What personal values will you bring to the team and what do you want to get out of it?

Connect to our **AMBITIONS**... *our goals!*

We aim to create and maintain a shared understanding and team focus on the mission, vision, goals and strategies throughout the team life cycle. It is about making it possible for each and everyone within the team to understand and strive in the same direction, and through dialogue emotionally connect to the rational objectives.

Optional Tools:

Questions to reflect upon could be:

1. *How do we ensure that within the team we have a shared view on the business case?*

2. *How do we ensure that all stakeholders are clear on and share the team objectives?*

3. *What will it take for us to constantly prioritize and reach all stakeholders' shared ambitions?*

4. *How shall we work to ensure that our team ambitions are shared throughout the whole team life cycle?*

Connect to **US**... *our values and behaviours!*

The objective is to create a shared foundation for the team spirit, built on the team's collective beliefs, principles and values with agreed wanted behaviours. Shaping an attractive and productive culture, built on trust, that will make our team a more effective and great place to work.

We also need to align our social structure (e.g., our organizational structure, decision-making process, recruitment criteria, follow-up focus, measurement systems, reward schemes, our heroes, etc.) with our wanted team values and beliefs.

Optional Tools:

1. Team Core Values & Wanted Behaviour p. 123
2. From CVA to Action .... p. 129
3. Values in Action .... p. 143
4. My Team's Level of Trust .... p. 152
5. The Elephant in the Room .... p. 157
6. From Conflict to Creativity .... p. 160

Questions to reflect upon could be:

1. *What are the shared values that we need for us to be successful in our team?*

2. *What are the values that create motivation and spirit in our team?*

3. *What behaviours will be critical in our interactions with the stakeholders to our team?*

4. *How do we ensure that we constantly align with our desired values and behaviours?*

5. *How is our level of trust within our team? Is it healthy and productive or does it need to be addressed?*

6. *How well is our current social structure aligned with our desired values and beliefs to make it possible for everyone to behave in a desired way?*

7. *Among all the teams I belong to, what is unique about this team for me? What would motivate each of us to give more of our time to this team vs. other teams?*

Connect to our **LEARNING**... *how we grow and develop!*

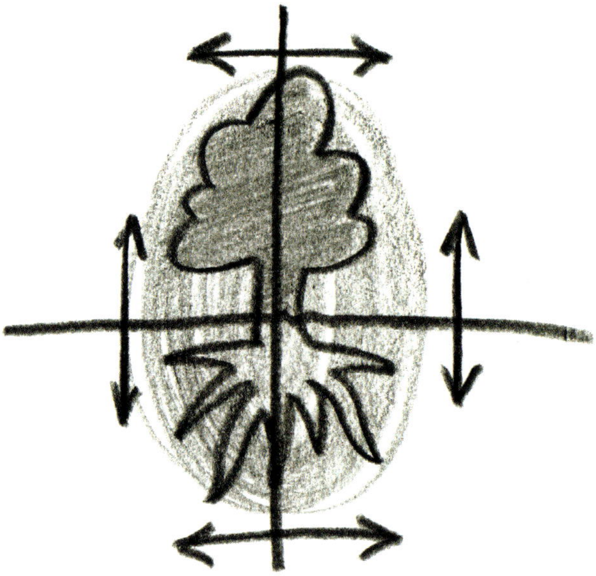

The purpose is to agree and create an environment for continuous reflection, transformation and learning throughout our daily work.

Learning and development are not only essential to our individual motivation and growth, but also to our agility and competitiveness as a team. How we work to learn and develop from our individual and collective experiences must be a natural part of our team culture.

Optional Tools:

Questions to reflect upon could be:

1. *How shall we work to bring the collective team knowledge and experiences to the surface and benefit from it?*

2. *How can we learn from our experiences during our daily operations?*

3. *How do we ensure that we recognise and affirm each other's individual and collective contributions (behaviours and results)?*

4. *How do we ensure that we give ourselves enough time to connect?*

5. *In what way could this team contribute to my personal and professional growth?*

4

IN PRACTICE

You may think, "Well this is a nice concept, but how do I make it all happen in my team?" First of all you have to accept the fact that you are dealing with the subjective intangible aspects of life when you wish to address, influence and grow a desired culture in a team. In practice this means that you need to understand that you are dealing with something that is often not so rational, logical and predictable.

A culture is influenced and based on human needs and emotions that are constantly moving and changing. In order for you to work practically with your culture you must define your current reality, so that you can start your journey from where your team is now.

This chapter describes a few practical perspectives that impact team culture development:

- Team vs. Working Group
- Dynamics of Power
- Management vs. Leadership
- Cultural Heritage
- Operational process and culture
- Directions of Energy
- Rational and Emotional Phases
- To measure and grow your culture
- Assessment of needs

These perspectives are chosen because we know they have a great impact on your culture and thereby your team performance. The way you realize, understand and are able to connect to these perspectives enables you to determine your current culture status and challenges. Read and use the self-reflective questions to get a better understanding of your current team culture.

There is also an alternative approach at the end of this chapter (page 56) which offers you a practical way to assess your needs together with your team. The assessment is based on the 'Get Connected' concept (Chapter 3) and it helps you to select the appropriate questions and tools to work with your team.

Working with your culture takes time and it needs consistent and persistent attention and care. In practice this means that you as the leader of your team need to make sure that culture is a natural part of your daily working agenda. What you give attention to and talk about grows.

TEAM VS. WORKING GROUP

The word of team is used loosely in today's workplace to define a variety of structures when a group of people are working together under a set of goals and objectives. Yet most of the so called "teams" do not qualify as teams but working groups only. A team must exhibit a minimum set of behaviours, such as co-operation, information sharing and team work, which is built on a foundation of shared vision, values and positive relationship qualities. There is an element of bonding within a team, both on a rational dimension and an emotional plane.

It is not necessary to always strive to build a team, a working group may be more appropriate under certain circumstances, such as working together for short term projects or to complete simple operational tasks. The importance thing is to first decide if you need a team or a working group. You then set realistic expectations among its members, call a spade a spade and not use the label of team to confuse matters and relationships.

If a team is necessary, then the team leader must put time aside to think through how to build it and make conscious choices about its developmental pathway. "What is in it for me?" is an essential question for a team leader to contemplate on behalf of each team member. To build a strong team, the factor of "what is in it for me" must be strong both at a rational level and an emotional level for each member. A team leader may need to make the tough choice of who should be on the "bus" to start with, to ensure there is a solid foundation for shared motivations. A sidelined team member could be quite destructive if left unattended and derail the morale of the whole team. To hold people together, a team must be strengthened through its activities and must be given the space to grow continuously. It has to be a live and growing entity to keep its vitality and performance. Nowadays, everyone is time poor and tries hard to eliminate waste activities, a team should not waste people's valuable time but energise its members through each interaction. If people start to make excuses and not show up for team meetings, a team leader must stop driving his/her goals, and must start team building. On the contrary, if people choose to drop other activities and priorities to go to your team meetings, then your team is strong and you are cooking with gas.

What is the current reality of this team? Is it a team or a working group?

What are the compelling reasons for us to build and sustain a team? What time, energy and resources would this process take?

What is the level of engagement of each member? Who should be on the bus; who should be off?

What holds this team together? How does each member rates the level of bonding of this team vs. other teams they are part of?

How does this team behaviour align with timelines and deliverables? What is their passion and how are they developing?

DYNAMICS OF POWER

The "what is in it for me" factor is often linked to and amplified by the structure of power, i.e. who holds the authority over each member, who the stakeholders for the outcome of this team are and what strategic importance in the organisation this team holds. The power structure, both formal and informal, sets the tone for the motivations of a team as well as its operational context, and often has a key impact to the success or the failure of a team.

The formal reporting line is a typical stream of power. The team leader who has singular, formal authority over his/her members could demand time and attention from his/her team, and may consider strengthening the reporting power line with leadership qualities. When there are dual or multiple reporting lines involved for team members, a team leader must carefully consider the underlining power dynamics and formulate effective influencing strategy. Good leadership by itself is not enough. Asking people to go extra miles without good pay back shall not sustain, and may be experienced as manipulation over time.

One common challenge for the development of a team culture is the culture of the organisation it belongs to and the power structure of this organisation. In a highly hierarchical organisation, formal power structure is a critical success factor for an effective team. In large organisations, there is often the power tension between centralisation vs. localisation, group structure vs. functional structure and direct line vs. dotted line etc. A team leader needs to be realistic with its operating environment and be mindful of the impact this team has on its members in their power status within the power structure of an organisation. The power dynamics include formal power status, influence level of key stakeholders, potential recognition involved and general look good factors. The team leader needs to actively link the work demand from this team to the strategic outcomes of key stakeholders, and continuously look after and even promote the "look good" factors for the team members involved. This is important for all sorts of teams, be it direct report or cross functional as well as intact or new.

What is the power hierarchy in our organisation? How does that impact the operation of my team?

Who are the key stakeholders for the success of my team? How could I engage them to promote the strategic importance of our team?

How could I effectively influence this team? What is the power dynamic within my team?

How do I give back to my team members? What can I do to make them look good?

MANAGEMENT VS. LEADERSHIP

In order for a team to be successful, we need to go beyond just managing the goals, the gates and the deliverables. Growing a healthy team culture with a strong and shared sense of direction and values will call for leadership skills rather than only management skills. Managers tend to focus more on time, quality and cost, making sure we meet the defined goals and deliveries. In contrast, leaders give more attention to set directions, motivating and aligning people to a shared purpose, helping them to grow and develop and to feel valued, resulting in a stronger sense of belonging and meaning.

Leaders are also conscious of their own values and behaviours and what impact these will have on the people around them. Leaders make sure they walk the talk and lead by example. That is why the 'Get Connected' concept not only addresses the team collective aspect but also enables you as a leader to connect to yourself. To be genuine and align what you think and feel with what you say and do.
A strong recommendation for you who have the role of building and leading of a culture is to start with yourself before you bring this to your team. This will not only connect yourself within but also give you a better understanding and confidence when you lead your team through the exercises.

Remember though, you do not need to be an expert to connect your team and grow a desired culture. All you need to do is to do the right thing by people for people and trust the process. Invest in circle time, set the stage, listen and be open to what happens, and make sure you reflect and learn from it. But do not be afraid to call for help. Ask consultants (internal or external) to come and facilitate dialogue sessions with you and your team, when needed.

What is your dominant leadership style – Manager, Leader or both?

What are your core motivations, vision, mission and values? How may these influence you in your role as a leader?

CULTURAL HERITAGE

Everyone has a history with different traditions, patterns, habits, etc that has shaped us. Your parents, schools, friends and the country that you grow up in shape your fundamental beliefs, values and principles, which in turn impact your attitudes and behaviours. You could call this our cultural heritage. It forms part of our "filters" from which we see the world around us. It could be of importance to pay attention to our individual and collective cultural heritage when trying to understand your current culture.

In many cases when we talk about 'culture' we think only of our country cultural origin or ethnicity. For example, "Swedes are very consensus driven – their decisions are always unclear", or "Koreans do not have any clearly expressed opinions – they are always so quiet". These quick judgments are based on stereotypes. These often very wrong assumptions can cause a lot of confusion and wasted energy in a team.

Nevertheless, it is important to recognise our country cultural heritages in order to understand, accept each other and work better together. If your team consists of members from different countries, then you need to invest in gaining awareness of the different country cultures. It is of great benefit that everyone understands their own country culture and themselves in relation to it before they start to learn about each other.

Remember when you invest in your culture you must start in defining your desired culture (vision, mission and values). Then you can invest circle time to understand each other's cultural heritage, for example our country culture. The other way around, it will most likely divide rather than unite your team.

> "To reduce time and space for reflection in development work, depletes the innovative ability, vitality, and in the long run also competitiveness. (Max Rapp Ricciardo, 2001)

What are the cultural heritages that impact you and your team's way of working?

OPERATIONAL PROCESS AND CULTURE

It is necessary and important to have well defined operational process describing the different project phases. A well-defined process with clear milestone targets helps enable all stakeholders to get connected to the project and to focus attention on the right issues at the right time. By doing this we also shape a culture built on the belief that having good order and discipline as part of all our tangible and rational project issues will make a successful project.

But such a process does not help us with everything that we need to grow and create an attractive and competitive project culture or healthy and efficient working climate. We have to understand that our structure is only an outcome of our beliefs and principles. To attain the desired culture we need to view it as based on our shared beliefs, values and principles. And since this is dependent on the human dynamics and not the predefined structure it can be illustrated by the level of relationship tension in a project.

See the conceptual illustration below;

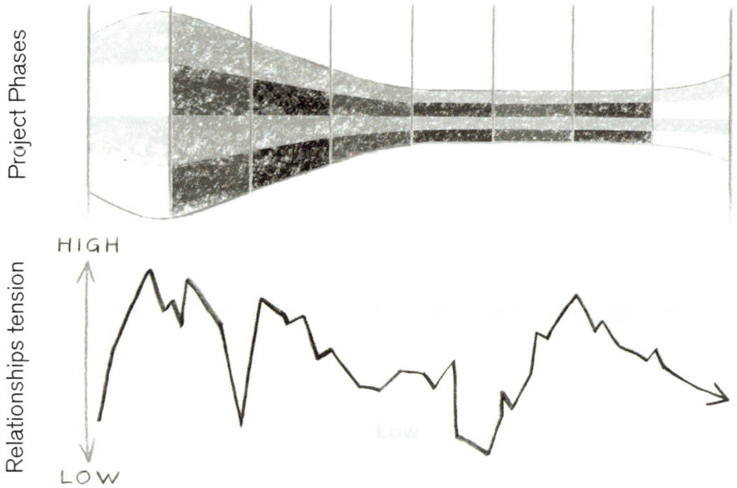

In the beginning of a project it is very common that we have higher relationship tension due to the fact that the people in the team have not connected to each other and the task yet. To reduce the relationship tension to a healthier level we need to invest in some dialogues where we can connect. However, high relationship tension is not always negative. It could be quite productive and constructive to have a high relationship tension, provided that it is built on mutual trust amongst the team members. A tension based on uncertainly and disrespect will never be effective.

What current level of relationship tension do you feel that you have with your team today?

Are you all aligned and pulling towards the same direction?

What are your shared values at this moment? What values and behaviours are currently at play and are they the same as your desired values? Are there any gaps?

DIRECTIONS OF ENERGY

A team culture can also be defined by its energy. Where and how you place your individual and collective energy tends to get the focus and priority. What captures our attention and what do we tend to prioritize and focus on? It would be best of course, if everyone in the team focuses their attention on the shared task we are all here to do. But we know that things happen that take our attention off the task. Below, are some typical examples of scenarios and challenges that could occur at different stages of a team, and that have an impact on the direction of energy. Use them to identify what challenges there might be on your agenda at this moment, and to determine what questions or tools would help to connect your team on an individual or collective level:

Getting people "on board":
- Selecting your team members
- Introducing new team members
- Agreeing on shared objectives
- Integrating people and task

Poor alignment:
- Conflict(s) within team, with customer, with Steering Committee, with the line organisation
- Conflicting needs/demands
- Lack of trust among stakeholders
- Your stakeholders don't share the same agenda
- Different view on deliverables
- Conflicting requirements/directives
- Lack of aligned line management commitment

Lack of energy and flow:
- Team members unhappy – leave the team
- Lack of motivation or/and drive
- Attitude problems – morale is low
- Energy level fades out
- Lack of initiative and involvement

Communication problems:
- Lack of open and honest communication
- The team members and/or different sub-teams do not co-operate/communicate
- Information hoarding
- Relationship conflicts and / or political agenda leading to blame and manipulation in communication

What is the energy direction in your team? What do you tend to focus your attention on?

Do you have positive and high energy in your team? Why/why not?

RATIONAL AND EMOTIONAL PHASES

The culture is unique for every team and every situation in any projects or initiatives. This is why we need to understand that it is not enough to only initiate but also to grow our desired culture. We also need to constantly review, nurture and develop our current culture during the whole process a team remains together, as well as throughout the different phases it goes through.

Clearly, projects go through phases when passing through defined gates in the project management process of an organisation. But these different phases often call for new tasks and challenges to reach our final goals and in many cases also call for new members with new ideas, and beliefs and values. These changes will also impact the subjective side of your reality and thereby the group dynamics, energy and flow. It is important to recognise that these types of emotional phases do not always follow one's predefined and planned visible phases. They are instead more governed by our emotional and spiritual state, but could still be defined even if they may be intangible and invisible for our eyes.

We have chosen to use two existing models that may be well known to you already. However, by reviewing your own team in relation to these models, you will better recognise your current team dynamics and culture and determine what desired culture would be relevant for you and your team to grow.

FIRO Model

One method of defining the phases that a team goes through is the FIRO model (Fundamental Interpersonal Relations Orientation) developed by the American psychologist Will Schutz.

According to the FIRO Theory, a group goes through the following development stages over and over again throughout its life cycle:

1. The Inclusion stage

The Inclusion stage is the first development stage of a newly established group. All members in the group are very anxious about being accepted by the others or about whether they really want to belong and adapt themselves to the group. Other common questions are how well they fit into the group and who the others are. The norms within the group, how to communicate and the different roles, are still unclear.

1b. The transition phase - "artificial cosiness"

This phase offers a short pause for breath, a sort of rest before the demanding role-searching stage. The members still try to please the others as they are feeling more relaxed with and are getting more and more engaged in the group.

2. The Role Searching stage

This stage is the most demanding in the group development process and takes the longest time to get through. The members of the group are no longer quiet, confrontations and trials of strength appear constantly and the disputes are normally about knowledge, leadership and competence. Sub groups are often formed, the atmosphere can be obviously aggressive and questions arise regarding who the leader is, how much influence each person has and how your competence is utilized.

2b. The transition phase – "idyllic atmosphere"

Before the next real stage a shorter phase of relief appears. The underlying conflicts come to the surface, the group starts to develop a common identity and the group members begin to understand their roles.

3. The Opening stage

Now the group functions as a unit and the members can focus their energy on the common goals. The group members are getting closer to each other, the atmosphere is more open and the prerequisites to manage problems that arise have improved. The members of the group reflect over what the others think of them, who they have the closest relations with and what level of openness and tightness in the relationships is allowed.

The group will sooner or later go back to a new Role Searching stage. If problems are not solved in a stage there is a risk that the group reverses one or more stages. The introduction of a new member or when groups are merged, are examples of when a group goes back from the Opening or Role Searching stage to the Inclusion stage again.

Tuckman Model

The Tuckman Model talks about team development phases as FORM – STORM – NORM – PERFORM. A team gets together around a shared purpose (they FORM). When they start to work they realize that they have different perceptions of the project's ambitions and on how to reach them, which creates tension in the team (they STORM). After some time they reach a more shared understanding and respect for each other (they NORM) and their productivity and ability to work together functions well (they PERFORM). This is illustrated in the picture below.

Research shows that successful teams do not FORM to STORM, instead they STORM to FORM. In practice this means that they invest in activities to un-

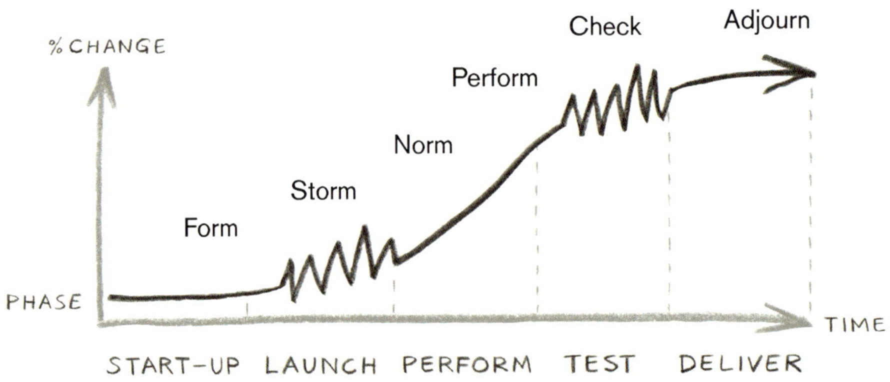

derstand and connect to each other's personalities, ambitions, etc. up front. The exercises presented in this book give guidance as to how this is carried out. You need to do regular checks to connect to your team and where they could be in their development. This is essential if you would like to know where to start and what to do in order to grow your team's wanted culture.

What emotional phase is your team currently in? What is your expected next phase and what impact will it have on your performance?

What is the desired emotional phase for you to effectively achieve your goals/objectives? How big is the gap and what are your leverage points to move your team forward?

TO MEASURE AND GROW YOUR CULTURE

Just as there are many ways to plan and execute a strategy, there are many ways to plan and deliver a cultural transformation program too. Barrett Values Centre provides models and tools for how to measure and grow a desired culture, called CTT (Culture Transformation Tools).

This process is based on a few fundamental principles, like "What gets measured gets done (and can be managed)", and "Cultural transformation starts with individual transformation (especially the leader)". At the same time it is important to recognise that this process is only a start, and in order to grow a desired culture you need to be prepared to work consistently and persistently with your culture over a longer period. Sometimes it can take years to get your culture to where it needs to be. Or, even more rightly it is a never ending story to work with your culture. Having said that, the process presented below provides you with a great start, and could also serve as a way to constantly follow up and review your cultural evolution.

By measuring the values you can make the invisible culture visible. This is done by collecting the perception of values and behaviour in your team. However, it takes almost no time to set up and measure your culture, but the important part of this "journey" is the way on how you work with the results after the measurement.

The intention here is to provide a high level outline of these steps so that you can understand what and how you could measure and grow your culture with the use of CTT. To work with CTT you need to be a trained user, or work with a CTT Certified consultant. However, you could also use the tool "Core Values & Wanted Behaviour". This does not provide you with all the information about your culture, but good enough to get you started. The tool "From CVA to Action" gives a more detailed description of the steps to take.

Here is an overview of the 6 basic steps for using a Cultural Values Assessment (CVA) and working in a practical transformation process.

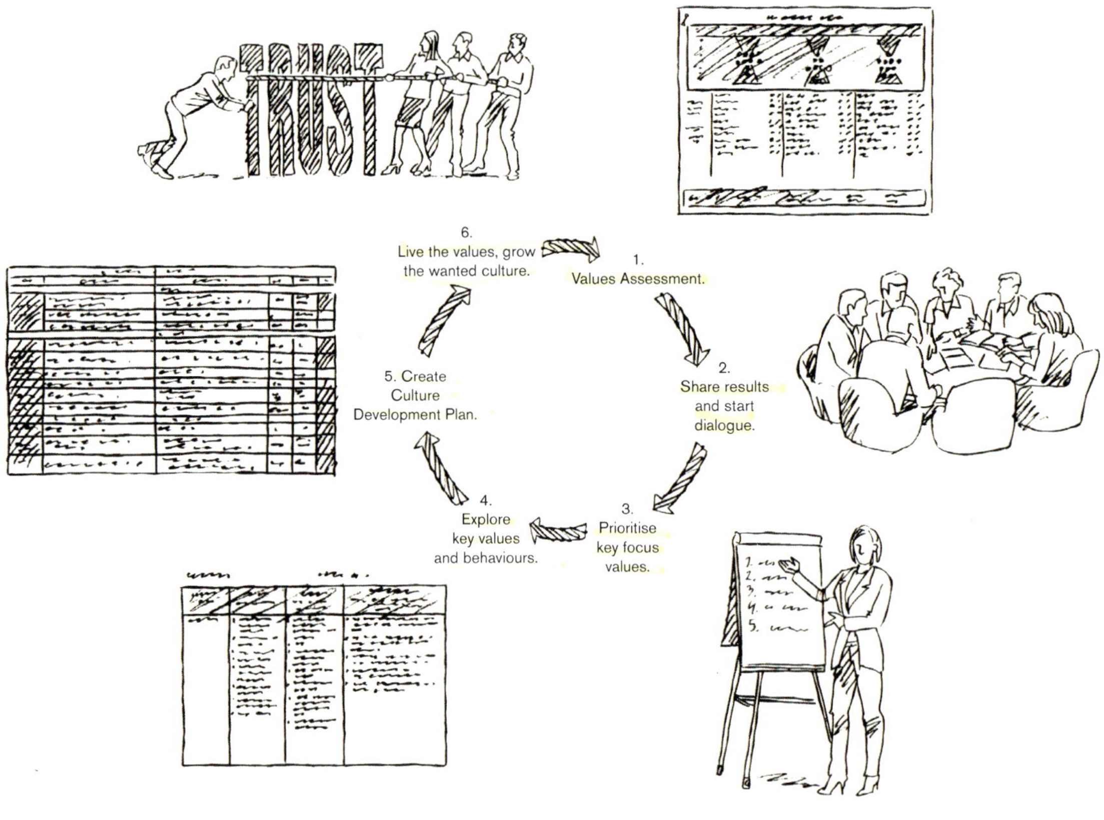

1) Values Assessment (All employees)

Contact a certified CTT consultant to help you set up the CVA survey. Usually you need to start 3-5 weeks before you want to have a report. In this preparation you will define and adjust the values list to be used, the demographic cuts you would like to see, and languages to be used.

The assessment is done on-line via a website and takes normally 15-20 minutes to answer. The benefit here is that you can (which is recommended) ask and involve all members in your team and/or organisation. There are three simple questions asked:

Question	What this tells us
1. Personal Values - Please select ten of the following values/behaviours that most reflect who you are, not who you desire to become.	The values that are important to your people in their personal lives? This is vital data that allows you to build a culture where people feel they belong.
2. Current Culture - Please select ten of the following values/behaviours that most reflect how your team / organisation currently operates.	How do your people experience the team / organisation now? What is working well? What is undermining engagement and performance?
3. Desired Culture - Please select ten of the following values/behaviours that you would desire for your organisation to achieve high performance.	What your people believe are the next steps (values and behaviours) to drive engagement and performance.

Within 5 days after the survey has closed you will get the report via mail in Word and PowerPoint.

The example on the right shows the 2012 values assessment for Barrett Values Centre. You will notice that the current culture includes all 4 of the organisation's core values. (see page 55) This is a sign that the values are alive and well and form the basis for daily decision making. It is also a strong indication that the leaders are walking the talk.

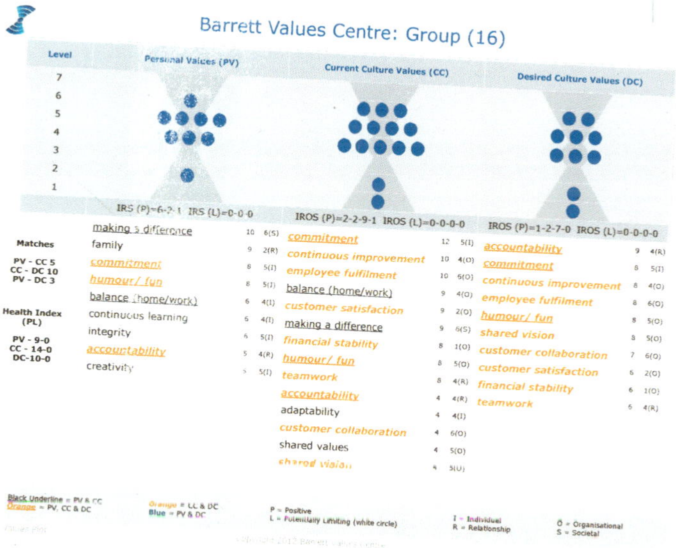

2) Share the results and start the dialogue (All employees)

The values assessment results are just a start point for a conversation. Now you need to invest circle time to sit and open a real dialogue. Listen to ideas that all your employees have to improve the way you work together. Help them to solve their own problems and frustrations. Your cultural transformation starts right here, at this moment in this conversation. The way to listen and involve and build in trust into this conversation will lay the foundation to your desired culture.

Here are some questions to help open the inquiry:

- What are the good news / what is to celebrate in these results?
- What challenges, problems, frustrations does this show? (Dig deeper to get examples and allow people to speak openly.)
- What is missing?
- What are the requests for transformation that become clear and what are your ideas to bring them to life?

3) Prioritise key focus values or choose Core Values

If your organisation or team does not have a set of core values, this could be good input to choose and define your core values that you want to become the foundation of your culture.

If your core values are already defined then you have an opportunity to see if they are really being lived. It may be time to focus on some new values and behaviours to take your teamwork and performance to the next level, and/or to better align your culture with your strategy. The following steps will then be based on exploring, developing and living those values.

4) Explore key values and behaviours (All employees)

Use the worksheets on page 140 to engage your people in a dialogue to explore the core values (or new focus values). Work in smaller groups of 3-5 people, with one value at the time. Remember that the dialogue is not only to reach an agreement of actions; it is more to help your team to form a shared understanding and bond together around what they have defined as important to best work together, and what motivates and gives them energy.

Type	Prioritized Actions	Follow-Up(How)	By Whom	By When	Progress
		Limiting Values			
1. Long Hours	1.1 Managing long hours within acceptable and agreeable level (Less than 20% of normal working hours)	a) Regular review in a weekly manager meeting b) Intensive analysis on previous month's O/T performance (Staff) including personal interviews	KH Lee	. Weekly . Monthly	
	1. 2 Efficient time management with individual task prioritization and optimization	a) Listing all "things to do" every morning (or weekly or monthly)before starting work & Prioritizing	All	. Immediately	
	1. 3 Having con. call during working hours as much as possible	a) Co-planning meeting schedule considering Korea time zone	All	. Immediately	
		Desired Values			
2. Work & Life Balance	2.1 Creating "Charter of Work & Life Balance" for each person (Define, Develop, Review)	a) Reviewing on a regular basis (Bimonthly) & Introducing best practices to others b) Helping them achieve it through mentoring system	All Mentors	. By Aug.	
	2.2 Enhancing mind-set toward "Result Oriented"	a) Reviewing deliverable quality with constructive feedback by manager	Managers	. Immediately	
	2.3 Exchaging experiences and opinions with Mentors	a) Developing Mentoring system b) Sharing "Lessons Learned" within VITK	KM Koo	. By Aug.	
3. Open Communication	3.1 Be a good listener and humble from managers	a) Showing "Walk the talk" from manager in all contacts including meeting, personal visit, team building, mails etc.	Managers	. Immediately	
	3.2 Sharing information more and frequently	a) Sharing managers' meeting minutes b) Sharing financial performance c) Having a communication day	KH Lee SH Yong KH Lee	. Weekly . Quarterly . Quarterly	
	3.3 Improving individual ability to lead a meeting and to be an opinion leader	a) Giving employees more chances of being a moderator in a meeting	Managers	. Immediately	
4. Professional Growth	4.1 Achieving planned individual education objectives	a) Reviewing performance by manager on a regular basis	Managers	. Quarterly	
	4.2 Improving english ability	a) Institutionalizing english improvement & practice program (with foreigners, Perove etc.)	JH Chung	. On-going	
5. Customer Satisfaction	5.1 Enhancing mutual trust continuously based on our professional and proactive attitude	a) Follow-up on VITK specifics in the global Customer Satisfaction Survery (Like twin_team approach program) b) Regular meeting to review VITK performances defined both in the SLAs and management level	EY Kim	. By Aug . As defined in SLA	
	5.2 More listening and Quicker response from customer viewpoint	a) Weekly meeting b/w CIO & AM(Account Mgr) regarding pending issues b) Monthly meeting b/w CIO & VITK managers regarding customer IS/IT objectives	EY Kim	. Weekly . Monthly	

5) Create a Culture Development Plan

(Small team)

If you have a team that is more than 10 people, you need to select a cross-department team to create a simple and practical Culture Development Plan for the year. Their task is to develop a draft plan which you as a leader then can present, adjust and agree with your whole team. The input to the plan is coming from all the suggested behaviours and actions that emerged from the step 1-4 above. This is also a good time to make sure that these suggested actions are aligned with your customer promise and strategy. Ideally this should be short enough to fit on 1 piece of paper. See template on page 136.

6) Live the values and grow the wanted Culture (All employees)

The values must be woven into the day to day decision making and behaviours. It is critical that leaders walk-the-talk and set an example for everyone else. This will show people that you are serious and create new levels of trust.

Feedback is key! It reflects what you have your attention on and how you look at what is important to you. If team members are not living the values you must have the courage to challenge them and help bring them and their behaviours into the desired culture. As much as you constantly need to provide positive feedback, catching people doing things right!

Don't forget to celebrate along the way!

It is recommended that you plan for a follow up within 6 to 18 months (it depends: if you have a lot of energy leakages and dysfunction in your current culture you need to do follow up sooner). By measuring again, you will be able to see your progress and learn from what works and what still needs to be worked on. It also signals that you are concerned about your culture and that you are being consistent and persistent in your ambition to grow a better culture.

Barrett Values Centre - Values & Behaviours

This is a live example of a values statement that shows the work in action.

Value	Definition	Behaviours
Commitment	We bring a willing spirit to the work we do. We support the organisation in delivering our mission and vision. We are dedicated to performing to the best of our abilities, even in difficult circumstances.	• Deliver on promises and maintain high standards in all professional endeavours. • Go beyond the call of duty to benefit the greater good of the organisation, the network and the end clients. • Keep the Barrett Values Centre vision, mission and values front and centre in making decisions. • Bring issues to the table and suggest ideas for improving our organisation.
Customer Satisfaction	We are dedicated to serving our customers' needs. We strive to help our customers grow and learn by keeping them informed and providing innovative products and services. We seek to make the customer an extension of our own organisation and keep them coming back for more.	• Set expectations with customers, and then work to meet or exceed them. • Seek to continually improve our customer experiences. • Be open, realistic and honest with customers. Work to meet immediate needs and provide alternative solutions when obstacles arise. • Listen to customer needs and collaborate with customers in an effort to support mutual learning and growth.
Employee Fulfilment	We strive to align our personal and organisational motivations. We understand that people have a need to grow as human beings, to expand their horizons and to meet new challenges. We seek opportunities to nurture each employee's gifts and sense of purpose within the context of the organisation's needs.	• Seek to grow and develop professionally and personally. • Support co-workers in their personal or professional development. • Demonstrate respect in relationships with colleagues and customers. • Strive to maintain realistic goals that support balance between work and home.
Shared Vision	We understand where we are going and the strategy for how we are going to get there. This understanding serves as a guide for bringing each other along and ensures we are moving forward in an all-inclusive manner.	• Be aligned with the purpose of the organisation and understand how your work supports the vision. • Seek to build a collective understanding of how projects and initiatives contribute to the company vision and mission. • Align day-to-day goals, actions and decisions with the company strategy. • Advocate and demonstrate the company vision, mission and values to all customers and strategic partners.

ASSESSMENT OF NEEDS

One way to connect to your team's current status and energy is to do a dialogue-based assessment. By this you will find the specific needs that your team has today. You can choose to do this by involving either a smaller core of team members or the whole team as well as key stakeholders in a reflection session where you start by presenting the 'Get Connected' concept.

This is how you do the dialogue based assessment:

1. Hand out a copy of the whole of chapter 3 "The concept" to everyone to read before the reflection.

2. Divide your team into small groups of 3 - 4 people and ask them to define through dialogue which of the 'Get Connected' five areas that they feel they have a good connection to and where they need to improve.

3. Ask them to reflect on one or two of the questions that they find most interesting in the area they selected.

4. Get all groups together to share their reflections and find where you need to invest more circle time to get better connected as individuals and/or as a team.

5. Optional: Select appropriate tool(s) to work with to get better connected.

Another suggestion to get a picture of your team's level of connection is to let them read the whole book and select the reflection questions they feel are important to work with. Alternatively, you could get your team to do the same reflections via picture images such as visual explorer, see website: www.valuescentre.com/getconnected

5

DIALOGUE TOOLS

These tools have been written in a way that should make it possible for a team to take them on without any help from someone outside of the team. But if you feel that there are times when it would be better to have a professional facilitator or coach to support you do not be afraid to ask for help! Such help can release you from the burden of hosting the process and allow you to focus on your own participation in the process yourself.

Every tool is written in a way that can be easily copied and brought to the team to read and work with. Each tool consists of a short introduction, purpose and objective, what to do step by step, and includes handouts if needed.

Most of these tools take 30 – 60 minutes to complete, with some exceptions which may extend to half day, or even full day workshops.

There is no specific order in how to use them, but they do connect and could support each other. Together they give you a good foundation to grow a desired team culture.

When working with the tools, please try to put them into a larger context and in a plan that stretches over an extended period of time, e.g. 6 to 18 months. This will increase your ability to grow and maintain your desired culture.

This whole book, supporting slides and related material can be downloaded free of charge at www.valuescentre.com/getconnected. This site also contains information on how to contact coaches and facilitators.

The tools to Get Connected:

For our REALITY:

For ME:

For our AMBITION:

For US:

For our LEARNING:

STAKEHOLDER ANALYSIS

Session Leader Guide

A team always has other people who have a stake in the output or purpose of their work. They are called stakeholders, who all have their unique needs and demands, expectations and relationship with the team. To acquire a good picture of all the key stakeholders and their specific demands and expectations it may be wise to make a "stakeholder analysis".
The value created by the team can be viewed from different perspectives and it is sometimes almost impossible to foresee all demands and expectations without involving the key stakeholders in a dialogue or discussion to gain a better and shared picture of the present situation.

PURPOSE

To map, review, involve and define the requirements and expectations from the key stakeholders of your change initiative.

OBJECTIVE

At the end of the exercise everyone should have a clear and mutual view of your key stakeholders and their requirements and expectations.

TIME

You will need 45 minutes for preparation and first draft of the stakeholder analysis. After that it depends on how many stakeholders you will meet; estimate 30-60 minutes per stakeholder. Then you need about 60 minutes for analysis and planning.

BEFORE THE SESSION

1. Anchor the decision to do the exercise in your team.
2. Select participants and book a meeting room.
3. Decide whether you intend to use a guest speaker to introduce the workshop and/ or create the right atmosphere.
4. Send out an invitation at least two weeks before your meeting and include any 'prework ' material if you find it useful to come better prepared. Communicate purpose and objective, when, where, and who.
5. Select the slides you intend to use. Look for ideas and select the supporting slides at www.valuescentre.com/getconnected.
6. Make sure the meeting room is ready with all the material needed.
7. If you intend to use a meeting evaluation or reflection, have it prepared in advance. (see page 172)
8. Try to come at least 20 minutes before everyone else.
9. Write the Purpose, Objective and Agenda on a flipchart so that everyone can see it during your whole session.

DURING THE SESSION

1. Introduce the purpose and objective of this exercise.
2. Explain the need to identify our stakeholders and the requirements and expectations they have on us and our team or our performance.
3. Ask everyone to find a blank piece of paper to map out your key stakeholders. Start by writing yourself or your team in the middle of the paper.
4. Identify every person or group of persons you think has an interest in your team or performance. Who are most important? Number them in order of importance for you.
5. Use symbols such as "+", "-" or "?" to indicate if they are positive, negative or indifferent. How do they influence?
6. Define what requirements and expectations you have on them – and write what you think their demands are on you or our team performance.
7. ALTERNATIVE: Follow the same steps described above. However, rather than using just a blank piece of paper, you can plot your stakeholders on an Interest/Influence map as depicted below.

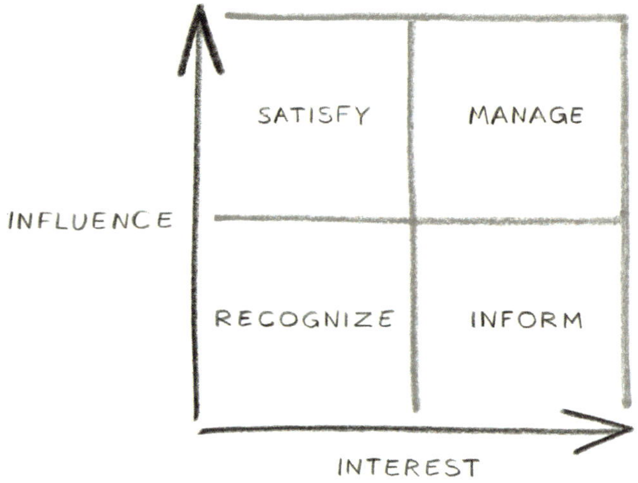

This will help you to better segment your stakeholders and to define strategies to handle them in the best way.

8. After everyone has completed their own personal stakeholder map, ask them to pair up in groups of 2 -5 persons. Share your maps, and identify and create one stakeholder map that describes your whole team. Ask each team to present their collective results. Collect each group's collective maps, in order to consolidate into a whole team map, if needed.
9. Invite them to a team reflection (see page 165) about the exercise. What has become clear to them? Any learnings, questions or concerns. Explain what the next steps are after this meeting. Any expectations from the team on the next steps?

AFTER THE SESSION

1. Make appointments with and meet all key stakeholders to check your relationship. The purpose with the meeting with your key stakeholders is to explore, rather than to explain. Have a dialogue about mutual requirements and agreements. What are the consequences of the discussion?
2. Make your analysis by yourself or preferably with your team. How should you handle the negative and positive forces? What will you do with conflicting requirements and expectations? Prepare your own action plan.

CONNECT TO THE CUSTOMER

Session Leader Guide

The more we can visualize the purpose of our work efforts in terms of how our solution will add value to our customer – the better we can understand and commit to the team goals. A good understanding of where our solution fits into the customer business operations and his/her intention and long term objectives will get us better connected to the customer and enhance the collaboration.

Additional benefits are that it can enhance the customer co-operation/dialogue, increase our ability to manage the customer requirements and enable us to work more proactively.

PURPOSE

To create a better understanding of how our solutions and performance will best contribute to the customer business operations.
To provide all stakeholders with an overall common purpose with the team, which will facilitate the customer cooperation/dialogue.

OBJECTIVE

A shared understanding and description of how the team connects to the customer vision and objectives in terms of Direction, Prerequisites and Dialogue.

PARTICIPANTS

The more team members that can participate the better. To provide value to the team, the minimum participants should be the team leader, 2-3 team members and customer representative(s).

TIME

The estimated time for this exercise is 3 – 4 hours depending on the size and complexity of the team and if it involves a visit to the customer premises.

BEFORE THE SESSION

1. Anchor the decision to do the exercise with your manager/chairman of the team and, where appropriate, with the Customer Account Manager.
2. Anchor the decision to do the exercise with your Customer.
3. Define who, when and where and book a meeting room.
4. Send out invitations at least two weeks before your meeting. Communicate meeting Purpose and Objective, when, where and who. Enclose the Agenda.
5. Prepare or select slides you intend to use
6. Make sure the meeting room is ready with all the material needed. You don't need more than a laptop, pc-projector and copies of the worksheets as handouts.
7. If you intend to use a meeting evaluation, have it prepared in advance (see page 172).
8. Try to come at least 30 minutes before everyone else.
9. Write the Purpose, Objective and Agenda on a flipchart so that everyone can see it during your whole session.

DURING THE SESSION

1. Present the Purpose, Objective and Agenda of the meeting. Highlight when you intend to end the meeting and ask if everyone will be able to stay during the whole meeting.
2. Introduce the exercise by reading out the steps to be taken. Clarify how you intend to use the material after the session. Make sure everyone understands the exercise. Give the opportunity for questions and concerns.
3. Make sure everyone gets the opportunity to voice his or her view. Be assertive and probe for questions. Remember, the process is as important as the outcome.
4. Conclude the exercise by reading out your final conclusions. Clarify agreed actions by addressing who, when and how. Communicate the intended next steps.

AFTER THE SESSION

1. Document the outcome of the workshop (use the template if appropriate).
2. Write and send out minutes as soon as possible after the meeting. Enclose the documentation with the outcome and also slides that were shown (if requested by any of the participants).
3. Now that you have started to create a shared understanding of how to get connected with the customer, plan for a dialogue with your team as to how to align the team behaviour and priorities.

Agenda

(proposal and facilitator notes)

1. Introduction of the exercise 15 min

2. "Guided tour" at the Customer premises (optional) 60 – 120 min

To create a better understanding of the current situation and the user priorities, meet the users of your products or solutions and view the physical environment where it will impact.

3. Individual Reflection 15 min

"Recall an occasion when you participated in a team where the collaboration with the customer was working perfectly." What made it happen? Who was involved? What was the feeling and outcome of this team?

4. Presentation of the Customer View 30 min

The customer presents Vision & Objectives, Priorities & Restrictions and Enablers & Critical Success Factors from his/her perspective.
Allow questions for clarification during the presentation.
Note down this information on flip chart(s). Put the flip chart(s) on a wall, where everyone can read it. (Use the template on page 65 if you want)

5. Group Reflection 60 min

"How can your team meet and connect to the Customer View?"
Note down the different responses on flip chart(s) under the heading "CONNECT" as they come up. Verify the responses towards the customer view and note where they are shared and agreed upon.

6. Evaluation of the Exercise 15 min

"How did the exercise contribute to a shared view and understanding of the team, priorities, prerequisites and dialogue?" What have we learned as individuals and as a team? What are the key issues to bring with us in our future work together?

7. Conclusion & End Up 15 min

Conclude the exercise by expressing your appreciation to the customer and the other participants.

HANDOUT

Connecting the Customer to the Team View

CUSTOMER Vision & Objectives	<-- CONNECT --> Why do we exist as a team?	TEAM VIEW Direction
Priorities & Restrictions	What do we need to pay special attention to?	Prerequisites
Enablers & Critical Success Factors	How should we create a cooperative working climate?	Dialogue

OPEN SPACE

Session Leader Guide

Working within an "Open Space" is meant to offer an open, creative exploration into topics that people choose to be relevant and important within a certain, defined, context. The agenda-items are often created on the spot. This, the open space facilitates a joint process for organizations and/ or groups to identify passions and concerns, share and learn from each others' experience to find meaning and creative approaches. The method works best in a situation when the following criteria are being met: a real need to explore, a diverse participation, complexity, both responsibility and passion (and/ or conflict) and a need to move on. This approach is not to be used when desired outcomes are already determined or when sponsors aren't prepared to take the meeting-outcomes into account.

PURPOSE

Open space offers a participative platform, where within a limited time-frame, a medium or a larger group of people, explores complex issues or a transformative topic and comes to deeper, shared understanding and potentially recommendations.

OBJECTIVE

At the end of this session this exploration might lead to a more connected picture of reality, shared understanding and sometimes recommended elements for building a new vision or a new approach, where multiple stakeholders will be taken into consideration.

TIME

The estimated time for this exercise is approx. 1 – 2 hours.

BEFORE THE SESSION

1. Prepare the session by exploring if/how it will contribute to a certain situation. It is important to ensure that the success-criteria are being met and that various stakeholders will participate during the session.
2. Define participant-group (there could be 20-1000) and book a meeting room with enough space to create a "market place": moving chairs around in order to sit in small groups and reporting back from different sides of the room. There should be numerous ways to capture information, for example on whiteboards or flipcharts.
3. Decide whether you or a guest speaker will introduce the workshop and/or create the right atmosphere.
4. Send out an invitation, communicate purpose and objective, when, where, and who.
5. Select the slides you intend to use. Look for ideas and select the supporting slides at www.valuescentre.com/getconnected or search the web for open space technology.
6. Make sure the meeting room is ready with all the support material needed.
7. If you intend to use a meeting evaluation or reflection-sheet, have it prepared in advance (see page 172).
8. Try to come at least 20 minutes before everyone else.
9. Write the Purpose, Objective and an agenda with time-schedule on one or multiple flipcharts so that everyone can see it during your whole session.

DURING THE SESSION

1. Present the purpose and approach of the meeting. Highlight when you intend to end the meeting. Ask if everyone will be able to stay for the whole meeting.
2. Ask the sponsor or manager to express his/her personal view on how important it is for each participant to clearly understand and articulate their view.
3. Introduce the exercise by sharing the 4 open space principles and the process steps to be taken.

   Speak about the open space principles and roles:
   a. Whoever comes to join your topic-group, are the right people.
   b. Whatever happens is the right thing
   c. When it starts is the right time; some groups might split and/ or start during the session, that is all welcomed: we do ask that the wall-agenda captures the groups/ topics, for people to be able to identify where the want to go (next)
   d. When it's over, it's over: there's no need to keep on talking if a group feels that the conversation has delivered the defined outcome;

   Then there's also certain roles and the law of two feet.

   The law of two feet: in case you feel that you need to move topic/ group, please do. This creates both butterflies (participants that go in and out of a session to individually reflect) and humblebees (someone "hopping" from one session to another, sharing ideas and insights between groups).

   Other roles are: an initiator or sponsor for the overall meeting, a convener: someone who calls a certain topic to be discussed and puts it on the agenda - often this person is also reporter for the conversation in that particular dialogue session.

   A report is created during/ after the dialogue and will be captured in some form at the end of the session.

AFTER THE SESSION

Make sure actions are taken to meet the reporting back and follow up on the commitments that came out of the meeting.

Agenda

(proposal and facilitator notes)

1. Introduction 15 min

Go through purpose, objective, principles and open a place for agenda-items to be posted. Be open for questions.

2. Small Group Dialogue 30 – 60 min

Form groups of 4-15 persons and ask the participants to share their thoughts and experiences around this topic, as well as invite ideas. Make sure that each participant is invited to share and point out that it is the dialogue itself that is as important as any outcomes.

Steps to take

- Present the small group approach and roles
- Open a "market place" agenda eg on the wall for topics to be posted
- Allow time (/a break) for people to form groups and define how long the dialogue sessions will take (eg 45 mins). Each of the groups to be in a visible place, preferably all in the same room.
- For the small groups the instruction needs to be that there is someone that facilitates the conversation and someone to capture the outcomes. Make sure everyone gets the opportunity to voice his or her view. Be assertive and probe for questions. Remember that the process of a joint sharing is as important as the outcome.
- Conclude the small group exercise with a shared reflection of the experience and learnings. Some groups prefer a creative reflection eg in the form of a visual, even a cartoonist or poet to shine a light on the work as well.
- Allow time in the plenary for a debrief of the experience. This could be a reflection on the process, comments from the audience, but is not necessarily a report from each of the small groups.

3. Whole Group Reflection 15 min

Have the group reflect on what was the major thing they learned and took away from this exercise?

IMPORTANT QUESTIONS

Session Leader Guide

Throughout life we all have good days and bad days. With everything going on around us in our daily work we all know that changes is a way of life, and we all react differently to change. As a team you either drive change or work to take on changes. It is very common that we judge the expected reaction from others based on our own thoughts and feelings.

During turbulent times of change or if you are unsure of what is going on "beneath the surface" in your team, you could make it a habit to ask these "Important Questions". This will give you and the team a better, updated picture of how your group feels and thinks at the moment, and we advise you start your meetings with these opening diagnostic questions especially when your team goes through more difficult times.

If you make it a habit of asking these questions even under "normal" times, it provides you and your team with a base for more connectivity and learning, and it will help to bond your team and make them more viable and independent.

The important questions are:

1. How are you feeling right now? How do you think your colleagues feel?
2. If any, what are your major "energy leaks" today? What about your colleagues?
3. What is the most important question for you right now?

PURPOSE

To create a better and mutual understanding of the group's present concerns, feelings and expectations. To surface individual and collective needs for action to deal with the current situation in the best way.

OBJECTIVE

At the end of this exercise you should be able to listen better and align your planned actions.

TIME

You will need 20-30 minutes, including the introduction, exercise and refection. The time will differ depending on how often you ask these important questions, the scope of the change your team faces at the moment, the level of trust in the group, etc.

STEPS TO TAKE

1. After completing the introduction phase of your meeting (e.g. Purpose, Objective and Agenda) you should explain the purpose of this exercise.
2. Write the three Important Questions on the whiteboard or flipchart.
3. Give everyone a few minutes to reflect individually on these questions and write down their answers on a piece of paper. After a while, encourage the group to share in pairs what they have written. Close by sharing your reflections with the whole group. Write key comments and conclusions on the whiteboard or flipchart so that everyone can read them.
4. NB! If the level of trust is low or has not been developed yet in the team, then have the team only discuss and share question number 3. Make the other two questions optional to share if they want to.
5. Take time to really understand what is being said. Ask for clarification and paraphrase to ensure that both you and your group have understood what has been said.
6. If the response and reaction is very strong to these questions, you may need to reconsider your original agenda and spend the rest of the meeting trying to understand and listening to the group's concerns. Remember, you do not need an answer to all questions. If you are unable to answer, say so. It is also important that you show integrity and are consistent in your beliefs and messages. The key purpose of the meeting is to listen and show you care.
7. Conclude the session by reading aloud your conclusions from what has been discussed and when and how you intend to revert to the issues. Be open to comments and adjustments.

AFTER THE SESSION

1. As the leaders of the team, reflect upon the outcome of what your team has shared. What are their key concerns, questions, dreams and desire at this moment? Where is their energy and focus? How do you need to respond as a leader to this? What actions, support and leadership is needed at this moment to take your team further and grow and develop?
2. Make sure the collected call for answers and actions are addressed (individually and/or collectively). Make sure you meet the expected commitments you have made.
3. Ask for help, if needed.

CORE MOTIVATION

Session Leader Guide

This exercise helps individuals and groups to discover what is important to them about their work and what motivates them at their deepest level.
The exercise is based on Richard Barrett's book "Liberating the Corporate Soul".

PURPOSE

To clarify the relationship between the team members' personal and organizational motivations.

OBJECTIVE

A shared understanding of what motivates the individual team members to bring their whole selves to work.

TIME

The estimated time for this exercise is approx. 1 – 2 hours.

BEFORE THE SESSION

1. Anchor the decision to do the exercise with the group.
2. Read through the whole Session Leader Guide – the best thing is to try out the exercises yourself first so you know the key steps.
3. Book a meeting room. Make sure that the room makes it possible to split up the group into pairs and work in pairs in an acceptable way.
4. Send out the invitations for your group meeting at least two weeks before your meeting. Communicate Purpose and Objective, when, where and who will be involved.
5. Select supporting slides to use at the workshop. Review speaker notes and add your own. You will find suggested slides at www.valuescentre.com/getconnected.
6. If you intend to use a meeting evaluation or team reflection, have it prepared in advance (see page 172).
7. Try to come at least 20 minutes before everyone else.
8. Make sure that you have printed hand outs for all participants.
9. Write the Purpose, Objective and Agenda on a flip-chart so that everyone can see them during the whole session.

DURING THE SESSION

1. Hand out the Core Motivation Exercise sheet to each person.
2. Instruct each person to fill in the answer to 'I go to work each day at__________because I want to ……' without using bullet points or itemised lists. One sentence only!
3. Once completed, have each person find a partner.
4. Partner B gives his or her sheet to Partner A. Partner A is then responsible for being the coach as well as the scribe for Partner B.
5. Have Partner A ask Partner B to complete the sentence "Why do you want to…*then read Partner B's sentence*…?" Partner A helps Partner B get clear as to what that answer is, then writes it down and reads it back for confirmation. Tell the participants that they can be probing their partner for a deeper meaning. Partner A also coaches Partner B in language and ideas. Focus shall be both challenge and support. Explore together!

6. They then change roles and repeat the process with Partner B interviewing Partner A.
7. Repeat the process a third and a fourth time if necessary until they are both satisfied that they have clearly and succinctly identified their respective core motivations. Once completed, the interviewing partner returns the paper to the interviewee.
8. The group reconvenes. Ask everyone to listen and hold back any comments. Voluntarily have each person read his or her answer that most accurately describes their core motivation. It does NOT have to be the last response on their paper.
9. Have the group reflect on the collective answers and what motivates us as a group and as indivduals.
10. Ask for comments on the process – what they felt, what they got out of the exercise.

AFTER THE SESSION

1. Write and send out any minutes as soon as possible after the meeting. Enclose the slides you showed (if requested by any of the participants).
2. How do you intend to follow up the session? A good idea is to plan a follow-up discussion and an individual follow-up at your annual performance review meeting with the participants.
3. Consider what steps you want to take next. For example the exercise "Personal 4 Whys" could be an appropriate exercise now while the group has a fresh experience of this exercise and thereby the thinking and emotions related to it.

Agenda

(proposal and facilitator notes)

1. Introduction of the exercise — 15 min

Go through Purpose, Objective and Agenda. Be open to questions.

2. Individual reflection of Core Motivation — 15 - 30 min

Distribute the hand-outs including the Core Motivation template and example. Ask the participants to reflect and note down their personal Core Motivation statement.

3. Completion of the Core Motivation statement — 30 – 60 min

Ask the participants to select a partner and let them complete the forms according to the instructions.

4. Group Dialogue — 15 min

Ask for volunteers to share their results with the larger group.
It is beneficial if everyone wants to do this.

5. Reflection — 15 min

Have the group reflect on what was the major thing they learned and will take away from this exercise?

HANDOUT

Core Motivation Question

I go to work each day at ______________________ because I want to:

PERSONAL 4 WHYS

Session Leader Guide

This exercise helps individuals in a group to create their personal vision and mission. The exercise is based on Richard Barrett's book "Liberating the Corporate Soul".

PURPOSE

To create mission and vision statements for the individual team members.
To clarify the relationship between the individual team members' personal vision and mission and how that can contribute to society.

OBJECTIVE

A shared understanding of the alignment between what motivates the individual team members and how they want to make a difference in society and in the world.

TIME

The estimated time for this exercise is approx. 1 – 2 hours.

BEFORE THE SESSION

1. Anchor the decision to do the exercise with the group.
2. Read through the whole Session Leader Guide – the best thing is to try out the exercises yourself first so you know the key steps.
3. Book a meeting room. Make sure that the room makes it possible to split up the group to work in pairs in an acceptable way.
4. Send out the invitations for your group meeting at least two weeks before your meeting. Communicate Purpose and Objective, when, where and who will be involved. If the group has done the Core Motivation exercise, ask them to bring the result to this exercise.
5. Select supporting slides to use at the workshop. Review speaker notes and add your own. You will find suggested slides at www.valuescentre.com/getconnected.
6. If you intend to use a meeting evaluation or team reflection, have it prepared in advance (see page 172).
7. Try to come at least 20 minutes before everyone else.
8. Make sure that you have printed sufficient hand outs for all participants.
9. Write the Purpose, Objective and Agenda on a flip-chart so that everyone can see them during the whole session.

DURING THE SESSION

1. Hand out the 4 Whys template showing the four quadrants of the model and explain what each quadrant represents.
2. Ask the team members to start to define their Personal Mission by answering the questions in the template. *a) What is your professional purpose?* and *b) What do you need to do in order to grow and develop as a professional?* Get them to write their answers in the form.
3. Ask the team members to select a partner with whom they will exchange their Personal Mission statements.
4. Let the partners interview each other on what each has defined as their respective Personal Mission.
5. The interviewing partner should start by asking question *c) Why do you want to fulfil your Personal Mission for yourself?* ....note the answer down as 'Personal Vision'. The partners then change roles so that the interviewer becomes the interviewee.
6. When each partner is satisfied that he/she has expressed their Personal Visions, they then repeat the process for the 'External Mission' by answering the question *d) Why do you want to fulfil your Personal Mission for your stakeholders/customers?*
7. When both partners are satisfied with their External Missions, again repeat the process for the 'External Vision' by answering the question *e) Why do you want to fulfil your Personal Vision and External Mission and bring benefit to society?*
8. Once the form is completely filled out, let the small group verify what they have defined. They do this by going through the statements in the opposite order, External Vision --> External Mission --> Personal Vision --> Personal Mission, changing the Why in the questions to 'How'. E.g. the answer to the question *e) 'How do you want to fulfil your External Vision and bring benefit to society?'* should be answered by the External Mission and Personal Vision statements.
9. Gather the team for a group reflection. Ask everyone to listen and hold back any comments. Have each person read his or her mission and vision statements.
10. Ask for comments on the process – what they felt, what they got out of the exercise.

AFTER THE SESSION

1. Write and send out minutes as soon as possible after the meeting. Enclose the slides you showed (if requested by any of the participants).
2. How do you intend to follow up the session? A good idea is to plan a follow up discussion and an individual follow up at your annual performance review meeting with the participants.
3. Consider what steps you want to take next. For example the exercise "Team 4 Whys" would be an appropriate exercise while the group still has this 'Personal 4 Whys' exercise, and also the thinking and emotions related to it, fresh in their minds.

Agenda

(proposal and facilitator notes)

1. Introduction of the exercise 15 min

Go through Purpose, Objective and Agenda. Be open to questions.

2. Individual reflection of Personal Mission 10 min

Distribute the handouts incl. the Personal 4 Whys template and example.
Ask the participants to reflect and note down their Personal Mission.
If the participants have done the Core Motivation and brought their result, they can use that result as the basis.

3. Completion of the 4 Whys template 30 – 60 min

Ask the participants to select a partner and let them complete the forms according to the instructions and example.

4. Group Dialogue 15 min

Ask for volunteers to share their results in the bigger group.
It is beneficial for everyone to do this.

5. Reflection 15 min

Have the group reflect on what was the major thing they learned and took away from this exercise?

Mission and Vision statements

Personal 4 Whys – Exercise

Personal Vision

c) Why do you want to fulfil your Personal Mission for yourself?

4. WHY? →

External Vision

e) Why do you want to fulfil your Personal Vision and External Mission and bring benefit to society?

↑ 1. WHY?

Personal Mission

a) What is your professional purpose?

b) What do you need to do in order to grow and develop as a professional?

2. WHY? →

↑ 3. WHY?

External Mission

d) Why do you want to fulfil your Personal Mission for your stakeholders/customers?

HANDOUT

Mission and Vision statements

Example

Personal Vision	External Vision
Answer the question what you as a professional want to fulfil. *To be widely acknowledged as a leading expert in Internet technology.*	Answer the question what your contributions will lead to for society. *To contribute to effective and efficient communication solutions, leading to energy savings and having a positive impact on our environment.*
Personal Mission	**External Mission**
Answer the question what you want to have your focus on and what motivates you professionally. *To design innovative web-based solutions.*	Answer the question what purpose you want your Personal Mission to have for your stakeholders/customers. *To provide world-class web solutions enhancing the communication abilities for my customers.*

Mission and Vision statements

Template

Personal Vision	**External Vision**
Personal Mission	**External Mission**

PERSONAL VALUES & HOT BUTTONS

Session Leader Preparation Sheet

The purpose of this preparation exercise is to help participants reach a better understanding of their own most significant personal values. The exercise does not only help you understand yourself better, it also offers the team the opportunity to voice their beliefs and values which is a critical part of building a stronger social capital and connection within a team.

When it comes to personal commitment and motivation, understanding your own personal values is more important than understanding your company core values. So it is recommended that you start with this exercise before you take the journey to identify and define your wanted team core values.

PURPOSE

To help participants reach a better understanding of their most significant personal values and to create a forum where a team can share these values in an atmosphere of understanding and acceptance. It serves as a foundation for alignment exercises.

OBJECTIVE

Identify your team's personal values and recognize what the team shares in common.

TIME

The estimated time for this exercise is approx. 1 – 2 hours.

BEFORE THE SESSION

1. Anchor the decision to do the exercise in your team.
2. Select participants and book a meeting room.
3. Decide whether you intend to use a guest speaker to introduce the workshop and/or create the right atmosphere.
4. Send out an invitation at least two weeks before your meeting and include the 'PREWORK' material. Communicate purpose and objective, when, where, and who.
5. Select the slides you intend to use. Look for ideas and select the supporting slides at www.valuecentre.com/getconnected.
6. Make sure the meeting room is ready with all the material needed.
7. If you intend to use a meeting evaluation or reflection, have it prepared in advance (see page 172).
8. Try to come at least 20 minutes before everyone else.
9. Write the Purpose, Objective and Agenda on a flipchart so that everyone can see it during your whole session.

DURING THE SESSION

1. Present the Purpose, Objective and Agenda of the meeting. Highlight when you intend to end the meeting. Ask if everyone will be able to stay for the whole meeting.
2. Ask the manager to express his/her personal view on how important it is for each participant to clearly understand and articulate their personal values as one of the starting points in our values journey.
3. Introduce the exercise by sharing the steps to be taken. Make sure everyone understands the exercise. Allow time for questions and concerns.

   Steps to take (alt. 1):
   - Bring up your prepared Personal Values & Hot Buttons.
   - Everyone share their top 3 personal values and descriptions (approx. 10 - 15 min per person). If it is a large group divide into groups of 2 - 4 persons.
     NB: Emphasise that the dialogue and explanations are the main goals of the exercise, not merely stating what your values are.
   - When everyone has shared their Personal Values, repeat the process with your Hot Buttons.
   - When everyone is finished sharing, ask for reflections; How did it feel? What did you think? What have you learned? Are there any concerns or questions?

   Steps to take if the team members have known each other for some time. (alt. 2)
   - Follow a similar procedure to Alternative 1. above, but with the difference that everyone has to guess what their team members have written as their Personal Values, based on the behaviours they have observed when working with them.
   - Depending on time available you could either guess or just share your Hot Buttons.

4. Explain the importance of understanding and being in contact with your own personal values and how this is linked to your company values.
5. Make sure everyone gets the opportunity to voice his or her view. Be assertive and probe for questions. Remember, the process is as important as the outcome.
6. Conclude the exercise by a reflection followed by what you expect to be the next step on your culture build-up journey.

AFTER THE SESSION

1. How do you intend to reinforce your team's reflections and conclusions (if any), and make your progress visible, that is, visual aids, questions, recognition, etc.?
2. Now that you have started to create a shared understanding of personal values and hot buttons, make sure your behaviour and priorities are aligned e.g. do we walk our talk?

Agenda

(proposal and facilitator notes)

1. Introduction 15 min

Go through Purpose, Objective and Agenda. Be open for questions.

2. Individual reflection of Prework 10 min

Ask the participants to bring up their Prework notes and take some minutes to reflect individually.

3. Small Group Dialogue 30 – 60 min

Form groups of 2 – 4 persons and ask the participants to share their personal values and descriptions. Point out that it is the dialogue itself that is most important. (Use alt. 1 or alt. 2)

4. Whole Group Reflection 15 min

Have the group reflect on what was the major thing they learned and took away from this exercise?

HANDOUT - PREWORK

Reflection on Personal Values

It is very important that you create a foundation for your own personal values. The following exercises will help you focus on this.

I. A LIFE VALUES EXERCISE

Other people have a great influence on our lives. John Donne said, "No man is an island." Martin Luther King spoke of the "web of mutuality."

Identify three people who have had the deepest impact on your life (at least one outside your family). What specific advice, philosophy, or value has stayed with you?

Name	Value

List three books, tapes, movies, poems, or sayings that have contributed to your own values. What insight has stayed with you?

Resource	Insight

Tennyson in Ulysses says, "I am part of all I have met." List three peak experiences that have profoundly shaped your life and/or career direction.

Experience	Value

NB! This part of the PREWORK is personal, and will not be shared with someone else, unless you want to.

HANDOUT - PREWORK

II. PERSONAL VALUES SELECTION

The purpose of this preparation exercise is to help you reach a better understanding of your own most significant personal values. It is beneficial to do this exercise every one or two years.

What values do I truly and passionately hold?

Values are deeply held views of what we find worthwhile. They come from many sources: parents, religion, schools, peers, people we admire, and culture. Many go back to childhood. There are others we learn as adults. As with all mental models, there's a distinction between our "espoused" values, which we profess to believe in, and our "values in action" which actually guide our behaviours. These latter values are coded into our brains at such a fundamental level that we can't easily see them. We rarely bring them to the surface or question them. That's why they can create dissonance for us.

Step 1. From the enclosed list of personal values, select the ten that are most important to you - as guides for how to behave, or as components of a valued way of life. Feel free to add any values of your own to this list.

Step 2. Now that you have identified ten, imagine that you are only permitted to have five values. Which five would you give up? Cross them off. Now imagine that you are only permitted four. Which would you give up? Cross it off. Now cross off another, to bring your list down to three. Then, do it again to bring your list down to two. Finally, cross out one of your two values. Which is the one item on this list that you care most about?

Step 3. Now that you have identified your three values, complete the exercise on page 87.

HANDOUT - PREWORK

List of Values

- ☐ accountability
- ☐ achievement
- ☐ adaptability
- ☐ balance
- ☐ being liked
- ☐ being the best
- ☐ caring
- ☐ caution
- ☐ challenge
- ☐ clarity
- ☐ commitment
- ☐ community involvement
- ☐ compassion
- ☐ conflict resolution
- ☐ continuous learning
- ☐ control
- ☐ cooperation
- ☐ courage
- ☐ creativity
- ☐ dialogue
- ☐ diversity
- ☐ ease with uncertainty
- ☐ efficiency
- ☐ enthusiasm
- ☐ environmental awareness
- ☐ ethics
- ☐ excellence
- ☐ experience
- ☐ fairness
- ☐ family
- ☐ financial stability
- ☐ forgiveness
- ☐ friendship
- ☐ future generations
- ☐ generosity
- ☐ health
- ☐ honesty
- ☐ humility
- ☐ humor/fun
- ☐ image
- ☐ independence
- ☐ initiative
- ☐ innovation
- ☐ integrity
- ☐ interdependence
- ☐ job security
- ☐ listening
- ☐ logic
- ☐ making a difference
- ☐ mentoring
- ☐ mission focus
- ☐ open communication
- ☐ openness
- ☐ optimism
- ☐ patience
- ☐ performance
- ☐ perseverance
- ☐ personal fulfillment
- ☐ personal growth
- ☐ philanthropy
- ☐ power
- ☐ pride
- ☐ professional growth
- ☐ quality
- ☐ reliability
- ☐ respect
- ☐ responsibility
- ☐ reward
- ☐ risk-averse
- ☐ risk-taking
- ☐ safety
- ☐ self-discipline
- ☐ spirit
- ☐ success
- ☐ trust
- ☐ vision
- ☐ wealth
- ☐ wisdom
- ☐ work/life balance

If you cannot find your preferred values above, please list your own below

☐ ____________________ ☐ ____________________ ☐ ____________________

☐ ____________________ ☐ ____________________ ☐ ____________________

Source: Barrett Values Centre

HANDOUT - PREWORK

III. Personal Values Statement

Based on the two previous exercises, list your top three values and describe what each value means to you.

Value	Personal Description
1.	
2.	
3.	

IV. Hot Buttons

Next, define your "hot buttons." A hot button has a deep root in one of your personal values. It is a behaviour or a situation that can make you feel very strongly because it crosses or goes against one of your personal values. For example, if one of my core values is honesty, then a hot button for me might be that I can feel deeply affronted if I discover that people are acting on hidden agendas. If one of my personal values is respect, my hot button might be when I see unfair public criticism by a manager of one of their employees. Even though we might share the value, we might still have different hot buttons. They are unique to each of us.

Describe at least one hot button for each of your personal values.

Value	Hot Button
1.	
2.	
3.	

FROM PVA TO ACTION

Session Leader Guide

A good start on your personal journey to get better connected to your personal values. There are many ways in which you can do this, Barrett Values Centre offer you two possibilities. One is to do an Individual Values Assessment (IVA), or a Personal Values Assessment (PVA). The difference between a IVA and a PVA is that a IVA provides a picture of your perception of the values at play at your workplace and the alignment or gap in between, while the PVA focus only on your personal values list. It is vitally important to know your values so that you can consciously use them in your decision making.

This tool is based on the self-assessment PVA. You find the on-line assessment at www.valuescentre.com/pva and it is a free of charge report. The report you receive analyses your top ten personal values to determine, a) the levels of consciousness you operate from, and b) the types of values that are important to you (individual, relationship, societal). It provides you with a framework to relate to your own values and determine your strengths and improvement areas, as well as your next step of evolution.

The exercise is based on one of the tools in The New Leadership Paradigm Workbook: Leading Self. You can learn more about this at www.newleadershipparadigm.com

It also works well to use an IVA as a base for this exercise, but then you need to work together with a certified CTT consultant. Go to www.valuescentre.com/partners to find a consultant near you. This exercise could be done individually as well as together with your team. The benefit of doing the exercise with your team members is that it provides an opportunity for you to get to know each other better on a deeper and more profound level. Which is fundamental when growing respect and trust between each other. It also offers you a possibility to get feedback and affirmation on your personal values and if you walk your own talk or not.

If you decide to do the exercise with your team, then we recommend that you ask your participants to do the PVA and personal reflections before the group meeting. Ask participants to bring their results with them.

PURPOSE

To find out more about yourself. What is important to you and what motivates you.

OBJECTIVE

To deepen your understanding of the values that are important to you and the levels of consciousness you operate from.

TIME

The estimated time for this exercise is approx. 1 – 2 hours.

BEFORE THE SESSION

1. Anchor the decision to do the exercise in your team.
2. Select participants and book a meeting room.
3. Decide whether you should prepare yourself or use a guest speaker to introduce the workshop and/or create the right atmosphere.
4. Send out an invitation, communicate purpose and objective, when, where and who.
5. Select the slides you intend to use. Look for ideas and select the supporting slides at www.valuescentre.com/getconnected.
6. Make sure the meeting room is ready with all the material needed.
7. If you intend to use a meeting evaluation or reflection, have it prepared in advance (see page 172).
8. Try to come at least 20 minutes before everyone else.
9. Write the Purpose, Objective and Agenda on a flipchart so that everyone can see it during your whole session.

DURING THE SESSION

1. Present the Purpose, Objective and Agenda of the meeting. Highlight when you intend to end the meeting. Ask if everyone will be able to stay for the whole meeting.
2. Ask the manager to express his/her personal view on how important it is for each participant to clearly understand and articulate their view.
3. Introduce the exercise by sharing the steps to be taken. Make sure everyone understands the exercise. Allow time for questions and concerns.
4. Make sure everyone gets the opportunity to voice his or her view. Be assertive and probe for questions. Remember, the process is as important as the outcome.
5. Conclude the exercise with a shared reflection of the experience and learnings.

AFTER THE SESSION

Make sure to recognize and see each other's strengths and behaviour as confirmation and acknowledgement of what you have shared with each other during your meeting.

There should only be individual actions after this exercise, no team actions, except the action defined above.

Individual Exercise

(Could also be used as instruction to be sent out via mail before a team meeting)

1. Get prepared 10 min

Bring paper and pen to make notes, if needed. Find a place where you can be undisturbed and by yourself for about 30-60 minutes. Connect to the PVA website at www.valuescentre.com/pva. Relax and get centred to be here and now. If you want, you could do the "Creative Mind – Meditation", which you find at page 190.

2. Do Personal Values Assessment 5 – 10 min

Select the values that most represent who you are, not who you would like to be. If you don't find your exact value word in the list, please select the one that best describes your personal value. Write your own value in your own notes, too. Complete the online survey, and get your report (pdf) via mail. Print your report and read it. Make notes of what becomes clear about you, and highlight what best describe who you are.

3. Analyse and reflect 30 – 45 min

Use the two worksheets in the PVA to reflect upon your most important values and behaviours and values you want to live and/or explore more. Share page 92 or 197.

4. Prepare (3-5 min) presentation 15 min

If you are going to have a team meeting where you will share your personal values, please prepare yourself to talk about your most important values and behaviours. You only have to share what you feel like sharing. No one can force you to share what you don't feel like sharing. You may also share what you want to explore or do more of, your individual evolution.

Agenda – Team sharing

(proposal and facilitator notes)

1. Introduction 20 – 30 min

Go through Purpose, Objective and Agenda. Be open for questions and concerns. Invite the participants to share how it was to do the individual exercise. Ask if there are any specific learnings, questions or concerns from the prework.

2. Sharing and listening 20 – 60 min

If you have a small team, ask everyone to stand in front of the group for a few minutes and describe their main results. If you have a larger group, split the group into threes and give them about 20 minutes to share and discuss their answers with each other.

3. Whole Group Reflection 15 – 30 min

Have the group reflect on what was the major thing they learned and took away from this exercise?

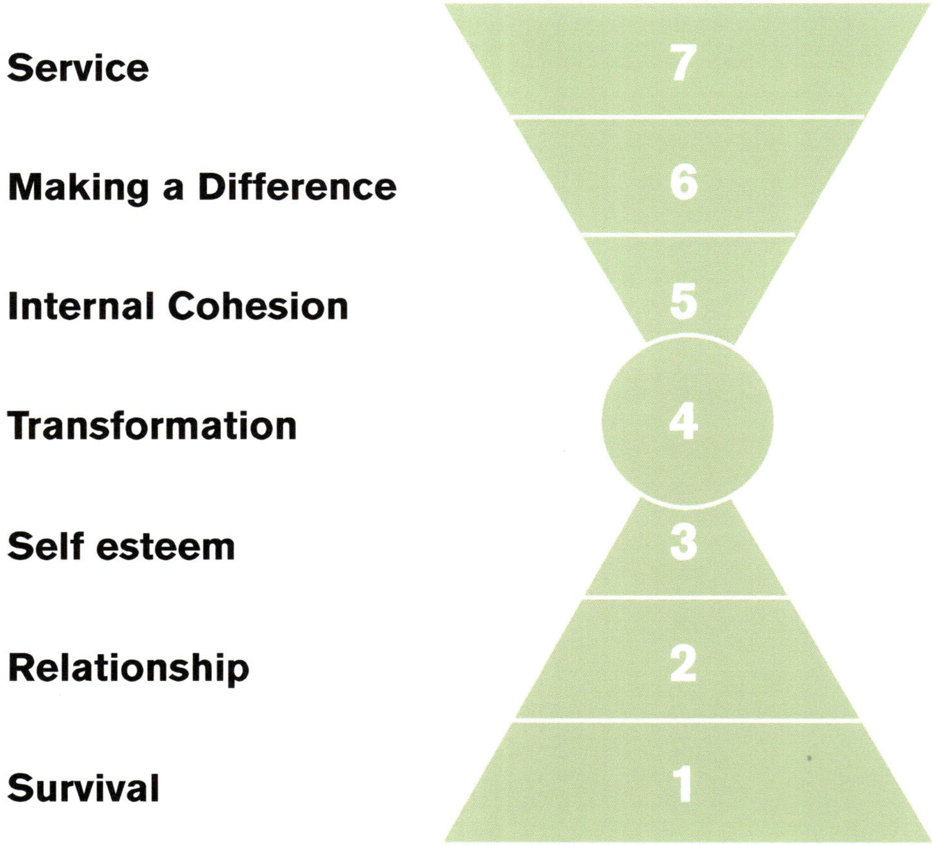

Positive Focus / Excessive Focus

Service to Humanity and the Planet
Devoting your life in selfless service to your purpose and vision.

Collaborating with Partners
Working with others to make a positive difference by actively implementing your purpose and vision.

Finding Personal Meaning
Uncovering your sense of purpose and creating a vision for the future you want to create.

Personal Growth
Understanding your deepest motivations, experiencing responsible freedom by letting go of your fears.

Self-worth
Feeling a positive sense of pride in self and ability to manage your life. Power, status.

Belonging
Feeling a personal sense of belonging, feeling loved by self and others. Being liked, blame.

Financial Security & Safety
Creating a safe secure environment for self and significant others. Control, greed.

FROM FEAR TO TRUST

Session Leader Guide

The purpose of this exercise is to help participants gain a greater understanding of fears that hold them back from courageous action and to create next steps to resolve a current problem situation. It can be used as a stand-alone exercise or used as a module in a longer workshop. All human beings experience fear. Fears have a very positive side, they help to keep us safe and enhance our chances of survival in dangerous situations. However, our fears can also hold us back from facing and exploring unresolved problems and relationship conflicts. Our fears are often sourced from negative childhood experiences or learned from the people (organisations and community) that we live within.

PURPOSE & OBJECTIVE

- To attain new understanding about difficult problems or relationship issues that are holding you back.
- To create the next steps necessary to find a resolution
- To explore the values, beliefs and behaviours (consciousness) that drives or restrains your actions.

TIME

The estimated time for this exercise is approx. 1 – 2 hours.

BEFORE THE SESSION

1. Anchor the decision to do the exercise with the group.
2. Read through the whole Session Leader Guide – the best thing is to try out the exercises yourself first so you know the key steps.
3. Book a meeting room. Make sure that the room makes it possible to split up the group into pairs and work in pairs in an acceptable way.
4. Send out the invitations for your group meeting at least two weeks before your meeting. Communicate Purpose and Objective, when, where and who will be involved.
5. If you intend to use a meeting evaluation or team reflection, have it prepared in advance (see page 172).
6. Try to come at least 20 minutes before everyone else.
7. Make sure that you have printed hand outs for all participants.
8. Write the Purpose, Objective and Agenda on a flip-chart so that everyone can see them during the whole session.

DURING THE SESSION

1. Present the Purpose, Objective of the exercise. Highlight when you intend to end the meeting. Ask if everyone will be able to stay for the whole meeting.
2. Introduce the exercise by sharing the steps to be taken. Make sure everyone understands the exercise. Allow time for questions and concerns.
3. Explain the importance of understanding the fears that unconsciously drive our beliefs and actions.
4. Facing and understanding our fears can be a personal experience. Sensitively ensure that everyone gets the opportunity to reflect and voice his or her insights and learning from this exercise. Remember, the process is as important as the outcome.
5. Conclude the exercise by a reflection followed by what you expect to be the next step on your culture build-up journey.

AFTER THE SESSION

1. Make sure to recognize and see each other's strengths and behaviour as confirmation and acknowledgement of what you have shared with each other during your meeting.
2. There should only be individual actions after this exercise, no team actions, except the action defined above.

Agenda

(proposal and facilitator notes)

1. Introduction 10 min

Go through Purpose, Objective and Agenda. Be open for questions.

2. Individual work and reflection 10 – 15 min

Ask the participants to complete the handout and work through the steps in the exercise individually. This is personal reflection time.

3. Small Group Dialogue 30 – 40 min

Form pairs and ask the participants to share their stories and insights.

4. Whole Group Reflection 20 min

Have the group reflect on what was the major thing they learned and took away from this exercise?

1. Choose a real work situation / relationship that you would like to improve but so far you have been unable to resolve.
   Situation: ....
2. Use the Want-Have Consciousness Matrix below to describe the situation in four sentences.
3. Fill the boxes in the consciousness matrix, answering each with a short statement (not a narrative).

1. In this situation, what I want that I have......	2. In this situation, what I don't want that I have......
3. In this situation, what I want that I don't have......	4. In this situation What I don't want that I don't have......

4. With regard to the situation you have chosen, this matrix is the structure of your consciousness. It exposes the thoughts and beliefs that inform your action or inaction.
5. To understand how this structure works, imagine that each cell is an internal Counsellor and the statement is his/her mandate.
6. Each counsellor has a 'positive intention' because they know what is good for you and has been a good partner to satisfy your needs.
7. It is important to understand what each Counsellor brings to you in this consciousness matrix.
8. In order to do so, create an imaginary conversation between the Counsellors behind each cell, as follows:
   - Notice what happens inside you when Cells 2 and 3 talk to each other...
     usually it is like an invitation to go forward ...because these are your "Driving Counsellors".
   - Notice what happens inside you when Cells 1 and 4 talk to each other...
     It is usually as an invitation to not move...because these are your "Restraining Counsellors".
   - Notice what happens inside you when the other Cells talk to each other...usually "internal conflict" arises...Cells 1 and 4 will fight to keep the status quo...because they are two very conservative Counsellors (they used to manipulate you with fear).
   - Avoid judging their responses and recognise the "positive intentions" of the four Counsellors that want to benefit you from their different perspectives.
   - Listen to their replies and connect with your feelings towards the working situation or the relationship you are dealing with.
9. What insights and understanding do you gain from this exercise?
10. What are the next steps you can take to address the unresolved situation and when will you act?

MANAGE YOUR ENERGY

Session Leader Guide

Our performance and actions depend on the individual level of energy in each of the members of a team or organisation. The more competitive the environment the greater demand it puts on us to deliver more in less time with fewer resources. This puts us under a lot of strain. In order to cope with these new demands in a productive and healthy way, we need to connect to our current level of energy and understand how and where we need to go to re-fuel.

Human beings need time to relax and recharge their energy, but are we aware of what it consists of and indeed, where we get our energy from? This tool has the ambition to help you to find your answer on these questions.

Our energy sources are strongly connected to our basic human needs. Physical, emotional, mental and spiritual needs. By assessing our perception of our current state regarding these needs we also get a good picture of what gives us energy and what changes we need to make to have a balanced energy management.

This tool is based on a Harvard Business Review article published in October 2007 by Tony Schwartz and Catherine McCarthy. It elegantly presents the challenges and possibilities with energy management in a short, simple, yet very useful way.
To find out more, please go to www.theenergyproject.com

PURPOSE

To create better understanding of, and identify our current individual level of energy and encourage us to work on it.

OBJECTIVE

Identify the areas I need to work on in order to improve my energy at work.

Have a picture of what you as a leader, and we as an organisation could do to better manage the energy in our teams.

TIME

The estimated time for this exercise is approx. 1 – 2 hours.

BEFORE THE SESSION

1. Anchor the decision to do this workshop in your team.
2. Define who, when and where and book a meeting room.
3. Send out an invitation at least two weeks before your meeting with purpose and objective and all practical details. Optional: Have the participants listen to Tony Schwartz talking about energy on the internet (www.theenergyproject.com).
4. Select the slides you intend to use. You need only your laptop, a pc-projector and the assessment template "Are you Headed for an Energy Crisis?" as handouts.
5. Make sure the meeting room is set up and ready with all needed materials. No special seating is needed. However, sitting in a circle without any table in front of you is recommended for better communication and connection.
6. Write the Purpose, Objective and Agenda on a flipchart so that everyone can see it during your whole session.

DURING THE SESSION

1. Present the Purpose, Objective and Agenda of the meeting. Highlight when you intend to end the meeting. Ask if everyone will be able to stay during the whole meeting, and/or if they need to have a break for e-mail or phone calls etc.
2. Introduce the exercise by reading out the steps to be taken.
3. Make sure everyone understands the exercise. Walk through the agenda (see proposal and facilitation notes at the end of this tool). Allow time for questions and concerns. Underline and agree upon confidentiality, ie "what will be said in this room stays in this room".
4. Make sure everyone gets the opportunity to voice his or her view. Be assertive and probe for questions. Remember, the process is more important than the outcome in this exercise.
5. End the exercise by reading out your final conclusions. Clarify agreed actions by addressing who, when and how. Communicate intended next steps.

AFTER THE SESSION

1. Write and send out minutes (if any) as soon as possible after the meeting. Enclose the slides you showed (if requested by any of the participants).
2. Make sure the planned actions and wanted behaviours will be followed up according to your shared plan.
3. How do you intend to reinforce your team's conclusions, and make your progress visible? Whatever you decide, make sure it happens.

Agenda

(proposal and facilitator notes)

1. Introduction 15 min

Go through Purpose, Objective and Agenda. Reflect together about how you relate to human energy, what it is and why it is important to pay attention to it.

2. Individual scoring of Energy 10 min

Hand out the two-sided assessment "Are You Headed for an Energy Crisis?"
Ask everyone to complete the assessment without sharing their scores with anyone else, unless you personally feel like sharing your results.

3. Reflect and connect to our Energy 30 – 60 min

NB! This step is only to be done if everyone feels comfortable in sharing their needs for energy in the team. If so, ask everyone to review their results and bring up what they feel is needed to be addressed in order to take better care of and create more energy in this team. Give everyone enough space and time to express their views and needs. Focus on listening, do not justify, correct or neglect the needs expressed. Look for themes in the dialogue, and check your assumptions. Note the shared themes on the flipchart or white board.

4. Next step and follow up 15 min

Encourage everyone to identify their own individual actions to improve their energy. Review the common themes and agree upon what actions you need to work on as a group. Discuss and agree on how you will reinforce, recognise and follow up. Set a date for review and follow up meetings.

5. Reflection 15 min

Have the group reflect on the following questions:

a. What was the major thing you learned and took away from this meeting?

b. What are the success factors to make our agreed actions happen?

HANDOUT

Are You Headed for an Energy Crisis?

Please check the statements below that are true for YOU.

BODY

- ☐ I don't regularly get at least seven to eight hours of sleep, and I often wake up feeling tired.
- ☐ I frequently skip breakfast, or I settle for something that isn't nutritious.
- ☐ I don't work out enough (meaning cardiovascular training at least three times a week and strength training at least once a week).
- ☐ I don't take regular breaks during the day to truly renew and recharge or I often eat lunch at my desk, if I eat it at all.

EMOTIONS

- ☐ I frequently find myself feeling irritable, impatient, or anxious at work, especially when work is demanding.
- ☐ I don't have enough time with my family and loved ones, and when I'm with them my thoughts are often on other things.
- ☐ I have too little time for the activities that I most deeply enjoy.
- ☐ I don't stop frequently enough to express my appreciation to others or to savour my accomplishments and blessings.

MIND

- ☐ I have difficulty focusing on one thing at a time, and I am easily distracted during the day, especially by e-mail.
- ☐ I spend much of my day reacting to immediate crises and demands rather than focusing on activities with longer-term value and high leverage.
- ☐ I don't take enough time for reflection, strategizing, and creative thinking.
- ☐ I work in the evenings or on weekends, and I almost never take an e-mail–free vacation.

SPIRIT

- ☐ I don't spend enough time at work doing what I do best and enjoy most.
- ☐ There are significant gaps between what I say is most important to me in my life and how I actually allocate my time and energy.
- ☐ My decisions at work are more often influenced by external demands than by a strong, clear sense of my own purpose.
- ☐ I don't invest enough time and energy in making a positive difference to others or to the world.

By Tony Schwartz and Catherine McCarthy

Self Scoring

HOW IS YOUR OVERALL ENERGY?

Total number of statements checked: __

GUIDE TO SCORES

0–3: Excellent energy management skills

4–6: Reasonable energy management skills

7–10: Significant energy management deficits

11–16: A full-fledged energy management crisis

WHAT DO YOU NEED TO WORK ON?

Number of checks in each category:

Body __

Emotions __

Mind __

Spirit __

GUIDE TO CATEGORY SCORES

0: Excellent energy management skills

1: Strong energy management skills

2: Significant deficits

3: Poor energy management skills

4: A full-fledged energy crisis

MY REFLECTIONS AND ACTIONS:

By Tony Schwartz and Catherine McCarthy

HANDOUT

***Tony Schwartz** and **Catherine McCarthy** recommend the following practices for renewing our four dimensions of personal energy:*

PHYSICAL ENERGY

- Enhance your sleep by setting an earlier bedtime and reducing alcohol use.
- Reduce stress by engaging in cardiovascular activity at least three times a week and strength training at least once.
- Eat small meals and light snacks every three hours.
- Learn to notice signs of imminent energy flagging, including restlessness, yawning, hunger, and difficulty concentrating.
- Take brief but regular breaks, away from your desk, at 90- to 120-minute intervals throughout the day.

EMOTIONAL ENERGY

- Defuse negative emotions—irritability, impatience, anxiety, insecurity—through deep abdominal breathing.
- Fuel positive emotions in yourself and others by regularly expressing appreciation to others in detailed, specific terms through notes, e-mails, calls, or conversations.
- Look at upsetting situations through new lenses. Adopt a "reverse lens" to ask, "What would the other person in this conflict say, and how might he be right?" Use a "long lens" to ask, "How will I likely view this situation in six months?" Employ a "wide lens" to ask, "How can I grow and learn from this situation?"

MENTAL ENERGY

- Reduce interruptions by performing high concentration tasks away from phones and e-mail.
- Respond to voice mails and e-mails at designated times during the day.
- Every night, identify the most important challenge for the next day. Then make it your first priority when you arrive at work in the morning.

SPIRITUAL ENERGY

- Identify your "sweet spot" activities—those that give you feelings of effectiveness, effortless absorption, and fulfilment. Find ways to do more of these. One executive who hated doing sales reports delegated them to someone who loved that activity.
- Allocate time and energy to what you consider most important. For example, spend the last 20 minutes of your evening commute relaxing, so you can connect with your family once you're home.
- Live your core values. For instance, if consideration is important to you but you're perpetually late for meetings, practice intentionally showing up five minutes early for meetings.

HOW COMPANIES CAN HELP

To support energy renewal rituals in your firm:

- Build "renewal rooms" where people can go to relax and refuel.
- Subsidize gym memberships.
- Encourage managers to gather employees for midday workouts.
- Suggest that people stop checking e-mails during meetings.

TEAM 4 WHYS

Session Leader Guide

This exercise helps individuals in a group to create their team vision andm ission and to clarify the connection to an external vision and mission for example to that of their customers and society. The exercise is based on Richard Barrett's book "Liberating the Corporate Soul".

PURPOSE

Through dialogue create mission and vision statements for the team.
To clarify the relationship between the team vision and mission and an external vision and mission.

OBJECTIVE

A shared understanding of the alignment between what is the purpose of the team and its contribution for a greater purpose e.g. for its customers and society.

TIME

The estimated time for this exercise is approx. 1 – 2 hours.

BEFORE THE SESSION

1. Anchor the decision to do the exercise with the group.
2. Read through the whole Session Leader Guide – the best thing is to try out the exercises yourself first so you know the key steps.
3. Book a meeting room. Make sure that the room makes it possible to split up the group in pairs and work in pairs in an acceptable way.
4. Send out the invitation for your group meeting at least two weeks before your meeting. Communicate Purpose and Objective, when, where and who will be involved. If the group has done the Personal 4 Whys exercise, ask them to bring the results to this exercise.
5. Select supporting slides to use at the workshop. Review speaker notes and add your own. You will find suggested slides at www.valuescentre.com/getconnected.
6. If you intend to use a meeting evaluation or team reflection, have it prepared in advance (see page 172).
7. Try to come at least 20 minutes before everyone else.
8. Make sure that you have printed handouts for all participants.
9. Write the Purpose, Objective and Agenda on a flip-chart so that everyone can see them during the whole session.

DURING THE SESSION

1. Hand out the 4 Whys template showing the four quadrants of the model and explain what each quadrant represents.
2. Divide into smaller groups, 3 – 5 persons in each group.
3. Present the questions:
   a) What is the purpose of our team?
   b) What do we need to do in order to grow and develop as a team?

   Give the groups the task to have a creative dialogue/brainstorming session, which should result in 1 - 2 statements that answer the questions and serve as a proposal for an Internal Mission.

4. List all proposed statements on a whiteboard or flip chart. Lead the whole team in a dialogue to select and agree upon which statements they feel most confident with as the Internal Mission. Get all participants to fill in the agreed Internal Mission in their forms.
5. Continue in the small groups to propose an Internal Vision by finding statements answering the question *c) Why do we want to fulfil our Internal Mission as a team and for our team members?*
6. Repeat the procedure in 4. above to reach agreement on an Internal Vision. Let all participants fill in the agreed Internal Vision in their forms.
7. Continue in the small groups to propose an External Mission by finding statements answering the question *d) Why do we want to fulfil our Internal Mission for our "customers"?*
8. Again, repeat the procedure in 4. to agree on an External Mission. Let all participants fill in the agreed External Mission in their forms.
9. Continue in the small groups to propose an External Vision by finding statements answering the question *e) Why do we want to fulfil our External Mission and Internal Vision and bring benefit to society?*
10. Again, repeat the procedure to agree on an External Vision. Let all participants fill in the agreed External Vision in their forms.
11. Once the form is complete, verify what they have defined by going through the statements in the opposite order, *External Vision --> External Mission --> Internal Vision --> Internal Mission,* but by changing the 'Why' in the questions with 'How'. E.g. the answer to the question *'How do you want to fulfil your External Vision and bring benefit to society?'* should be answered by the External Mission and Internal Vision statements.
12. Gather the team for a group reflection. Ask for comments on the process – what they felt, what they got out of the exercise and how they can individually connect to the result (see reflection questions in Team Learning).

AFTER THE SESSION

1. Write and send out minutes as soon as possible after the meeting. Enclose the slides you showed (if requested by any of the participants).
2. How do you intend to follow up the session? A good idea is to plan a follow up discussion 1 or 2 months after the session, and then at least one follow up annually with the team.
3. Consider which next exercises you want to conduct. For example the exercise "Team Core Values & Wanted Behaviours" would be an appropriate exercise now that the group has established their Vision and Mission statements.

Agenda

(proposal and facilitator notes)

1. Introduction 15 min

Go through Purpose, Objective and Agenda. Be open to questions.

2. Individual reflection 10 min

If the participants have done the Personal 4 Whys exercise, ask them to review the result and take some minutes for individual reflection.

3. Completion of the Team 4 Whys template 30 – 60 min

Divide into smaller groups of 3 – 5 people. Hand out the Team 4 Whys template and ask the groups to start to complete the form according to the instructions and example. For each area i.e. for Internal Mission, Internal Vision, External Mission and External Vision, gather the big group together to share their different outcomes. Have the big group agree on one common statement for each area.

4. Group Dialogue 15 min

Conclude by reading out the agreed Vision and Mission statements and ask for comments.

5. Reflection 15 min

Have the group reflect on the following questions:

What was the major thing you learned and took away from this exercise?

What are the success factors to make our agreed statement happen?

Mission and Vision statements

Team 4 Whys – Exercise

Internal Vision c) Why do we want to fulfil our Internal Mission as a team and for our team members? **4. WHY? →**	**External Vision** e) Why do we want to fulfil our External Mission and Internal Vision and bring benefit to society?
↑ 1. WHY? **Internal Mission** a) What is the purpose of our team? b) What do we need to do in order to grow and develop as a team? **2. WHY? →**	**↑ 3. WHY?** **External Mission** d) Why do we want to fulfil our Internal Mission for our "customers"?

Mission and Vision statements

Example

Internal Vision	External Vision
Answer the question on what the team wants to accomplish.	Answer the question on what contributions the team wants to make to society.
To be a world leader in Internet technology.	*To build opportunities for global economic prosperity.*
Internal Mission	**External Mission**
Answers the question on what the team wants to have as its focus, and what motivates the team members.	Answer the question on what services the team wants to give to its "customers".
To create and sell innovative web-based solutions.	*To provide world-class web solutions adding substantial value for our customers.*

Mission and Vision statements

Template

Internal Vision	External Vision

Internal Mission	External Mission

ALIGN STRATEGY & CULTURE

Session Leader Guide

There is a well know expression that "Culture eats Strategy, for breakfast". In reality this is very true, because even if you have the worked through and smartest strategy for your organization, it still will be very useless unless the culture in your team supports your strategy. If the people who are to execute and fulfill the strategy do not think and feel that they work in a healthy and trusting environment, then they will not have their focus on reaching your strategic objectives.

Strategy exists in the objective collective visible reality, often materialized in some form of strategy document with goals and targets. Culture on the other hand exists beneath the surface within each individual in their minds and emotions, which is invisible and quite often even subconscious. A culture starts by each individual becoming conscious of their own values and the collective values of your team and then this becomes visible in people's behaviors and performance.

However, culture needs strategy to survive! In order for a culture to live and prosper, the culture needs a shared ambition, purpose and direction. This is what a good strategy provides. So even if the culture could jeopardize your strategic ambitions, it still needs the strategy to survive. So the key is that you realize that you need both strategy and culture to free the full human potential!

The process to align your strategy with your culture is not as complicated as it may sound. Simply put, it is a conscious act of asking yourself what culture you need in order to reach your strategic objective. This tool provides you with these steps.

PURPOSE

To help you connect your strategy with a wanted culture that supports your strategic objectives.

OBJECTIVE

At the end of this session you should have realized your key challenges and identify behaviour and actions needed connected to each strategic objective.

TIME

The estimated time for this exercise is 1-2 hours.

BEFORE THE SESSION

1. Anchor the decision to do the exercise in your team.
2. Select participants and book a meeting room. Ideally it should be the leaders, but if a smaller team it could involve the whole team.
3. Decide whether you should prepare yourself or use a guest speaker to introduce the workshop and/or create the right atmosphere. Like your top leader, a customer, external speaker, etc.
4. Send out an invitation, communicate purpose and objective, when, where and who. Ask all participants to prepare themselves by defining what they regard as the prioritized strategic objectives the coming 12-18 months. Ask them to list them in short bullet points and in priority order. Ask them to print and bring their list to the meeting.
5. Select the slides you intend to use. What documents does your organization have to communicate your strategy? Slides, Word documents, printed leaflets, etc. Bring them! Look for ideas and select other supporting slides at www.valuescentre.com/getconnected.
6. Print the handouts, one for each participant.
7. Make sure the meeting room is ready with all the material needed.
8. If you intend to use a meeting evaluation or reflection, have it prepared in advance (see page 172).
9. Try to come at least 20 minutes before everyone else.
10. Write the Purpose, Objective and Agenda on a flipchart so that everyone can see it during your whole session.

BEFORE THE SESSION

1. Present the Purpose, Objective and Agenda of the meeting. Highlight when you intend to end the meeting. Ask if everyone will be able to stay for the whole meeting.
2. Ask the manager to introduce the workshop by expressing his/her personal view on how important this work is. And underline the importance for each participant to clearly share and articulate their view in an honest and open way, based on trust.
3. Introduce the exercise by sharing the steps to be taken. Make sure everyone understands the exercise. Allow time for questions and concerns.
4. Make sure everyone gets the opportunity to voice his or her view. Be assertive and probe for questions. Remember, the process is as important as the outcome.
5. Ask everyone to talk two by two about their expectations of this workshop. Then ask the team to share what they have talked about. Ideally, capture their expectation on a flipchart or white board so that everyone can see it. This is both to make everyone more connected to this work here and now AND for you as a session leader to hear and connect to their expectations.
6. Ask everyone to bring up their pre-work answer about the prioritized strategic objectives. Hand out the first handout and ask them to individually write down their answer to these two questions. When they are ready, ask them to talk about their answer in small groups of 3-5 persons.
7. Display the answers to the first question on a flipchart. Conclude if the displayed prioritized strategic objectives for the whole team are aligned and shared.

8. Share the challenges that have been identified in order to reach our strategic objectives. Try to define if these challenges are "hard/objective/tangible" challenges (above the surface) or "soft/subjective/intangible" challenges (below the surface). If possible display them on a white board, above or below a horizontal line like a waterline. The most common answer is that the most of the challenges identified are below the surface. See example below.

9. Look at the identified challenges and reflect upon "what does this tell us about our team and what we need to focus on to reach our strategic objectives?".
10. Hand out the second handout. Ask everyone to individually answer the two questions. When ready, share the answers in small groups of 3-5 persons. Ask them to reflect upon: When looking at the answers to question 1, what becomes clear to you? How do the identified values and behaviours align with the culture we have today? What are the major gaps? What proposed tools and actions have been identified? Ask them to prioritize 2-4 actions. What is needed to make this happen, and by when?
11. Collect and list all prioritized actions. Assign persons and resources, and set time.
12. Conclude the exercise with a shared reflection of the experience and learnings.

AFTER THE SESSION

1. Make sure actions are understood to meet the expectations of the commitments done at the meeting.
2. Include the follow up of the agreed actions into existing follow up meetings.

Agenda
(proposal and facilitator notes)

1. Introduction 10 min

Go through Purpose, Objective and Agenda. Be open for questions and concerns.

2. Our prioritized Strategic Objective and Challenges 30 – 60 min

Everyone present their prioritized strategic objectives.

3. Culture Values & Behaviours needed 30 – 60 min

Ask everyone to identify the values and behaviours, plus the tools and actions needed.

4. Whole Group Reflection 15 min

Have the group reflect on what was the major thing they learned and took away from this exercise.

Questions for reflection:

Your prioritized strategic objectives:

What are your biggest challenges to succeed in reaching your strategic objectives?

HANDOUT

Questions for reflection:

Based on your shared strategic objectives (for your organization as a whole, plus for your team in particular)...

1. What values and behaviours do you need to live by in order to reach your strategic objectives?

2. What tools and actions do you need to grow these values and behavior?

INTERNALISATION OF TEAM AMBITIONS

Session Leader Guide

Teams often have both direct and indirect consequences impacting a multitude of stakeholders. Awareness of the team's objectives and compatibility with the ambitions of the members and stakeholders is necessary to create a shared view and improve the level of consciousness from the key people needed to make the team successful.

This exercise sets out to raise a dialogue around the compatibility of team objectives with the ambitions of the key people needed to make the team successful.

You can do this on an individual level and/or a team level and the output from many of the other exercises within Get Connected can be used as input.

I.e. See the illustration below which shows the tools and exercises that can be used as input.

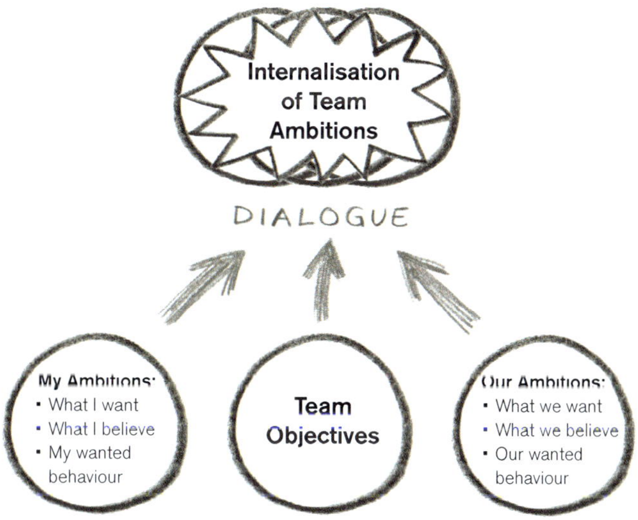

Optional Exercises
- Core Motivation
- Personal 4 Whys
- Personal Values
- PVA or IVA

Optional Exercises
- Connect to the Customer
- Stakeholder Analysis

Other Tools & Methods
- SWOT
- Objectives Modelling

Optional Exercises
- Team 4 Whys
- Team Core Values
- CVA

PURPOSE

To create a dialogue and bring to the surface, reflect upon and connect to the thoughts and feelings about our defined team objectives and deliverables.

OBJECTIVE

At the end of the exercise everyone should have a shared meaning and commitment to our team and deliverables.

TIME

Estimated time for this exercise is approx. 2 – 3 hours.

BEFORE THE SESSION

1. Anchor the decision to do the exercise with the group.
2. Read through the whole Session Leader Guide – the best thing is to try out the exercise yourself first so you know the key steps.
3. Optional: Run some or all of the optional exercises, tools and methods listed in the above illustration in advance so that their output can be used as input to this exercise. E.g.: Use Objectives modelling to break down the Team Objectives in to more manageable or meaningful parts. Use Stakeholder Analysis to understand and the various forces and agendas of Key stakeholders. Use the 4 Whys exercises to help bring to light the driving forces behind the team's motivation, etc.
4. Book a meeting room that makes it possible to work two by two in an acceptable way. Select supporting slides to use at the workshop. Review speaker notes and add your own. You will find suggested slides at www.valuescentre.com/getconnected.
5. Send out the invitation for your group meeting at least two weeks before your meeting. Communicate Purpose and Objective, when, where and who will be involved.
6. If you intend to use a meeting evaluation or team reflection, have it prepared in advance (see page 172).
7. Try to come at least 20 minutes before everyone else.
8. Write the Purpose, Objective and Agenda on a flip-chart so that everyone can see them during the whole session.

DURING THE SESSION

1. Follow the proposed agenda.
2. Present the model illustrated above showing My Ambitions, Project Objectives and Our Ambitions. Include the details relevant for you project and team. i.e. What are your project objectives? What personal or group ambitions have been identified so far? (Input from the optional exercises, tools and methods can be used for this).
3. Present the reflection questions and distribute the hand-out detailing them (included at the end of this exercise):
   - What becomes clear to me when I read/hear about our team objectives a ndeliverables?
   - How do I feel and think in relation to the team objectives and deliverables?
   - In light of the above, what will be needed in order to make this a successful team for all stakeholders and team members?
   - Do we understand and connect to the team objectives? If there are gaps, what are the Actions needed?
   - Where do we have a positive or negative energy focus? What actions are needed?

4. Divide the group into pairs and let them share their reflections/conclusions/concerns with their partner.
5. Gather the group again for a whole group reflection.
6. Have a team reflection on the alignment of their personal ambitions with the ambitions of the team, and what actions may be needed. Write down the team reflections and actions on a whiteboard/flip chart so that everyone can see and build on each other's reflections.
7. Let the team conclude what they find as critical for them in order to align their personal ambitions with the team ambitions. Try also to come to an agreement of how to follow up the agreed intentions e.g. by planning a follow up meeting.

AFTER THE SESSION

1. Write and send out minutes as soon as possible after the meeting is concluded. Enclose the slides you showed (if requested by any of the participants).
2. In certain cases follow-up meetings may be required to discuss compatibility of the team and personal ambitions. Examples:
   - In the case of a team member who becomes aware that his or her personal ambitions do not align with the team ambitions, a one-on-one discussion between that team member and their team leader may be needed to identify a workable solution. I.e. Can an adjustment be made to the person's role or responsibilities to better align ambitions?
   - One or more important stakeholders may realise there are clashes in ambitions. Are follow-up meetings required to re-clarify or redefine scope?

Agenda

(proposal and facilitator notes)

1. Introduction 15 min

Go through Purpose, Objective and Agenda. Be open for questions.

2. Reflection in small groups 30 min

Ask the participants to select a partner and share their reflections/ conclusions/ concerns with their partner.

3. Group Dialogue 30 – 60 min

Make each small group share their reflections and conclusions in the big group. Let the group reflect over what has been presented and share their opinions of what actions they feel are needed to get aligned with the team ambitions.

4. Reflection 15 min

Have the group reflect on what was their major learning and take-away from this exercise?

HANDOUT

Questions for reflection:

1. *What comes clear to me when I read/hear about our team objectives and deliverables?*

2. *How do I feel and think in relation to the team objectives and deliverables?*

3. *In light of the above, what will be needed in order to make this a successful team for all stakeholders and team members?*

4. *Do we understand and connect to the team objectives? If there are gaps what are the action needed?*

5. *Where do we have a positive or negative energy focus? What actions are needed?*

AI TO FREE COLLECTIVE ASPIRATIONS

Session Leader Guide

The collective "wisdom of the crowd" is more powerful than each individual wisdom. By using the basic principles of Appreciative Inquiry, we collect the positive wisdom to free our full human potential and build a shared commitment of our collective ambitions of behaviors connected to our desired values. You can use any values you desire to clarify with this tool.

PURPOSE

To surface and define the teams desired values behavior through a co-creating positive dialogue.

OBJECTIVE

At the end of the session have a shared view of the behavior we expect and want for each of our core values.

TIME

The estimated time for this exercise is approx. 2 – 3 hours.

BEFORE THE SESSION

1. Anchor the decision to do the exercise in your team.
2. Select participants and book a meeting room.
3. Decide whether you should prepare yourself or use a guest speaker to introduce the workshop and/or create the right atmosphere.
4. Send out an invitation, communicate purpose and objective, when, where, and who.
5. Select the slides you intend to use. Look for ideas and select the supporting slides at www.valuescentre.com/getconnected.
6. Make sure the meeting room is ready with all the material needed.
7. If you intend to use a meeting evaluation or reflection, have it prepared in advance (see page 172).
8. Try to come at least 20 minutes before everyone else.
9. Write the Purpose, Objective and Agenda on a flipchart so that everyone can see it during your whole session.

DURING THE SESSION

1. Present the Purpose, Objective and Agenda of the meeting. Highlight when you intend to end the meeting. Ask if everyone will be able to stay for the whole meeting.
2. Ask the manager to express his/her personal view on how important it is for each participant to clearly understand and articulate their view.
3. Introduce the exercise by sharing the steps to be taken. Make sure everyone understands the exercise. Allow time for questions and concerns.
4. Make sure everyone gets the opportunity to voice his or her view. Be assertive and probe for questions. Remember, the process is as important as the outcome.
5. Conclude the exercise with a shared reflection of the experience and learnings.

AFTER THE SESSION

1. Make sure actions are taken to meet the expectations of the commitments done at the meeting.

Agenda

(proposal and facilitator notes)

1. Introduction 10 min

Go through Purpose, Objective and Agenda. Be open for questions and concerns.

2. Select Value 20 min

Select the value to focus your attention on. The exercise "Team Core Values and Behaviour" or "From CVA to Action" could be used to identify your values.
You could also choose to work with one of your company espoused core values.

3. Story telling 45 min

Divide your team into breakout groups; ask them to share their personal stories about a time when they felt that our team or another company where they have been working displayed a strong sense of the value you have chosen. Make your description as lively as possible. Think of questions like:

- What was the situation?
- What were you doing?
- Who was with you?
- What was happening?
- How did the ability of your organization to develop a strong customer centricity make you feel?
- What was the most memorable aspect about this experience?

Give details.

4. Imagine 30 min

Imagine a time 5 years from now when everyone working in this team is a living example of your chosen value, either internal or external. Describe what would be happening in the team or in your organisation. What would it feel like? What would it look like?

5. Define concrete behaviour/actions 30 min

Within each breakout group, what does the above teach you on:

- What this value means for your work in your team and why it is important?
- Define: how will you operate (differently) to role-model this yourselves in the current environment in terms of your behaviour?
- Define some concrete goals/ steps/ actions, which you want to take in order to bring this value across more?

6. Share and agree follow up 30 min

In plenary: Share with the other groups your outcomes from step 5 and have dialogue about it. Appoint a "value-coordinator" to hold each other accountable for this in the coming months up to an evaluation point.

7. Whole Group Reflection 15 min

Have the group reflect on what was the major thing they learned and took away from this exercise?

Appreciative Inquiry

VALUE: SPECIFICS	BEHAVIORS

TEAM CORE VALUES & WANTED BEHAVIOURS

Session Leader Guide

This exercise helps you as a leader to establish a set of shared values and related wanted behaviours. To have shared values in a team will:

- create better understanding and communication.
- help people to function and work better together and feel better about what they do.
- create better co-operation and alignment of people towards a common goal.
- create the glue that keeps the team together.
- help to focus attention on the right issues.
- state the "fingerprints" of the organisation.
- create greater value for all the stakeholders.

Source: "The Leadership Challenge" by Jim Kouzes and Barry Posner

Clarifying what are the wanted behaviours related to the shared values, is fundamental when creating an effective and attractive work environment. The outcome from this exercise together with a shared vision and mission form a strong foundation for the team culture. Note that this is a learning journey, which demands continuous and consistent follow-up reflections and improvements to ensure that the team and its members walk-the-talk.

PURPOSE

Through dialogue to identify shared values, beliefs and wanted behaviours needed for an attractive and competitive team culture.

OBJECTIVE

To agree upon a shared list of values, supported by clear definitions of wanted behaviours.

TIME

The estimated time for this exercise is approx. 2 – 3 hours.

BEFORE THE SESSION

1. Anchor the decision to do the exercise in your team.
2. Select participants and book a meeting room.
3. Decide whether you should prepare yourself or use a guest speaker to introduce the workshop and/or create the right atmosphere.
4. Send out an invitation, communicate purpose and objective, when, where and who; include the list of values and ask each person to select three (3) values that they personally would see as guiding values for the team. Ask them to return their selected values one week before the exercise.
5. Collect the selected values from all participants and rank them in order of the number of "votes" each value received. i.e. the most selected value first, etc.
6. Select the slides you intend to use. Look for ideas and select the supporting slides at www.valuescentre.com/getconnected .
7. Make sure the meeting room is ready with all the material needed.

8. If you intend to use a meeting evaluation or reflection, have it prepared in advance (see page 172).
9. Try to come at least 20 minutes before everyone else.
10. Write the Purpose, Objective and Agenda on a flipchart so that everyone can see it during your whole session.

DURING THE SESSION

1. Present the Purpose, Objective and Agenda of the meeting. Highlight when you intend to end the meeting. Ask if everyone will be able to stay for the whole meeting.
2. Ask the manager to express his/her personal view on how important it is for each participant to clearly understand and articulate their view.
3. Introduce the exercise by sharing the steps to be taken. Make sure everyone understands the exercise. Allow time for questions and concerns.
4. Divide into smaller groups, 3 – 5 persons in each group.
5. Hand out the list of ranked values to each group and ask them to select and agree upon 3 – 5 values from the list. Use the enclosed template to define the meaning of each selected value.
6. Gather all the groups and let each group present their selected values. List the values on a whiteboard or flip chart.
7. Lead the whole combined group in a dialogue to reflect on the proposed values, then select and agree upon 3 – 5 of these.
8. Give the small groups some minutes to reflect on what these values mean in terms of behaviour(s) and propose actions to grow their desired culture.
9. Lead the whole group in a dialogue to agree upon which wanted behaviours are related to the selected values, how to make them come alive and finally how to ensure that the team members live their values. Note everything down on the whiteboard/flip chart or directly in the template on a PC with a projector.
10. Make sure everyone gets the opportunity to voice his or her view. Be assertive and probe for questions. Remember, the process is as important as the outcome.
11. Conclude the exercise with a shared reflection of the experience and learnings.

AFTER THE SESSION

1. Document the agreed values and behaviours and send it out as a draft to all participants. Ask the team members to reflect individually on whether they can commit to what was agreed at the exercise. Attach examples of how to visualize the selected Values and Wanted Behaviours.
2. Bring the result and comments to a short dialogue at the next team meeting to finally agree and create an Action Plan.
3. Make sure to come back to your core values and wanted behaviour in your daily meetings, by reading them and before you start and/or have a short reflection at the end of your meetings to conclude if you live by them or not. As a result of this reflection confirm the alignment or adjust.

Culture Values

- ☐ accountability
- ☐ achievement
- ☐ adaptability
- ☐ appreciation
- ☐ balance (physical/ emotional/mental/ spiritual)
- ☐ being the best
- ☐ caution
- ☐ celebration
- ☐ challenge
- ☐ clarity
- ☐ commitment
- ☐ community involvement
- ☐ compassion
- ☐ competence
- ☐ conflict resolution
- ☐ consensus
- ☐ continuous improvement
- ☐ continuous learning
- ☐ control
- ☐ co-operation
- ☐ cost consciousness
- ☐ creativity
- ☐ customer collaboration
- ☐ customer focus
- ☐ customer satisfaction
- ☐ diversity
- ☐ ease with uncertainty
- ☐ efficiency
- ☐ employee fulfilment
- ☐ employee health
- ☐ employee recognition
- ☐ empowerment
- ☐ enthusiasm
- ☐ equality
- ☐ ethics
- ☐ excellence
- ☐ experience
- ☐ exploitation
- ☐ fairness
- ☐ financial stability
- ☐ forgiveness
- ☐ future generations
- ☐ global perspective
- ☐ goals orientation
- ☐ honesty
- ☐ human rights
- ☐ humor/fun
- ☐ image
- ☐ information sharing
- ☐ innovation
- ☐ integrity
- ☐ interdependence
- ☐ internal competition
- ☐ job security
- ☐ leadership development
- ☐ listening
- ☐ long-term perspective
- ☐ loyalty
- ☐ making a difference
- ☐ mentoring
- ☐ mission focus
- ☐ open communication
- ☐ openness
- ☐ optimism
- ☐ organizational growth
- ☐ partnerships
- ☐ passion
- ☐ patience
- ☐ personal growth
- ☐ philanthropy
- ☐ power
- ☐ productivity
- ☐ professional growth
- ☐ professionalism
- ☐ profit
- ☐ quality
- ☐ recognition
- ☐ reliability
- ☐ respect
- ☐ responsibility
- ☐ results orientation
- ☐ risk-taking
- ☐ shared values
- ☐ shared vision
- ☐ short-term focus
- ☐ spirit
- ☐ strategic alliances
- ☐ support
- ☐ teamwork
- ☐ transparency
- ☐ trust
- ☐ vision
- ☐ wisdom
- ☐ work/life balance

If you cannot find your preferred values above, please list your own below.

☐ ____________ ☐ ____________ ☐ ____________
☐ ____________ ☐ ____________ ☐ ____________
☐ ____________ ☐ ____________ ☐ ____________

Source: Barrett Values Centre

Agenda

(proposal and facilitator notes)

1. Introduction 15 min

Go through Purpose, Objective and Agenda. Be open to questions.

2. Selection of values in small groups 30 – 60 min

Divide into smaller groups of 3 – 5 persons, hand out the list of ranked values and ask them to select 3 values and then to define the meaning of each value. Ask them also to describe how it appears when it works at its best and which wanted behaviours they would like to see in the team.

3. Group Dialogue 30 – 60 min

Gather them back into the big group and ask them to share their results from the previous step. Ask for comments and note them down. Try to coach the group in a dialogue with the ambition to reach a consensus as to which values and desired behaviours they want to have in the team. Continue and ask the group how they should make these values and behaviours come alive.

4. Agree 15 min

Ask the team if they can commit to live by these values and wanted behaviours from now on in the team. Ask also if they will accept to get reinforcing feedback if they live by them and redirective feedback if they don't live by them?
Agree when and how you and the team should follow up on your agreed values and wanted behaviours.

5. Reflection 15 min

Have the group reflect on what was the major thing they learned and took away from this exercise.

Value	**Definition** How do WE define this value?	**Culture** How does this value (behaviour) look like when at its best?	**Actions to Create** What actions can we* take to make this value grow? *) ME personally, WE as a group and the COMPANY / Management?

Example: Visualize your values and Wanted Behaviours

TEAMWORK

- *We actively contribute and share responsibility for results.*
- *We respect the opinions of each other and others and listens attentively.*
- *We ask for input and feedback from team members.*

TRUST

- *We are open and candid.*
- *We treat others with dignity and fairness.*
- *We operate with integrity and support colleagues.*

COMMITMENT

- *We deliver excellence in all professional endeavours.*
- *We can be counted on to deliver even in difficult circumstances.*
- *We keep mission, vision and values front and centre in making decisions.*

OPENNESS

- *We are proactive in taking initiatives to share information with each other.*
- *We bring issues to the table and speak honestly and openly about position and feelings.*
- *We support and encourage each other to engage in frank, honest and open conversations.*

CUSTOMER COOPERATION

- *We offer that little extra that the customers want, but don't actually think of.*
- *We have a positive attitude and tackle every job with enthusiasm.*

EMPLOYEE RECOGNITION

- *We recognize and appreciate good performance and desirable behaviours.*
- *We always strive to provide regular and positive feedback.*

TIP

Describe the values in terms of behaviour with an example or story.

FROM CVA TO ACTION

Session Leader Guide

This exercise is based on Barrett Values Centre's CTT (Cultural Transformation Tools) assessment called CVA (Culture Values Assessment). In order for you to work with these tools you need to be a trained CTT Consultant, or work with someone who is CTT certified user. If you need to get in contact with a certified CTT consultant, go to www.valuescentre.com/partners.

Organisational and team culture transformation begins with personal transformation, so if possible it is recommended that you combine this exercise with the exercise "From PVA to Action" on page 89. We especially recommend that you start with yourself first, if you are the leader of the team that you would like to transform the culture with. This will not only provide you with a better understanding and consciousness about yourself but also about the CTT language and tool to be used.

As we have learned that organizational transformation must critically start with, and be modeled by, the leader, this workshop is designed to help you initiate this process within your team. If you want to get a better overview of the whole process, then read "To measure and grow your culture" on page 52-55.

There is no "one-way" to run this type of workshop, so we have provided an alternative way for each of the steps for you to choose from to best fit your group and way of working. The important thing to remember is that you work in an involving and co-creating way. Regard this as an opportunity for you to engage and listen to and act upon what your team find important and value to make you as a team perform better together. Remember, the journey is as important as the end result and that when you decide to run this exercise you also start (or maintain) the cultural transformation journey in your team.

OBJECTIVE

To share and discuss the outcomes of a values assessment within your team, and to deeper explore the meaning and getting an in depth understanding of the values that people choose in the assessment. Then to:

a. Identify the key values and what they specifically mean
b. Describe the behaviours that do or would demonstrate the values
c. Celebrate what is right and examples of best practices that are already taking place
d. Agree causes and corrective actions of potentially limiting values
e. Distinguishing between quick win actions and a longer term direction of what the high performing culture should look and feel like.

TIME

The estimated time for this exercise is approx. 4-7 hours.

BEFORE THE SESSION

1. Anchor the decision to do the exercise with the group.
2. Read through the whole Session Leader Guide. Connect with a trained CTT consultant and agree on agenda and set up (make sure to plan time for this).
3. Book a meeting room. Make sure that the room makes it possible to split up the group into groups of 3-5 persons in an acceptable way. Make sure the room has the following:
   - PC projector.
   - Flip chart(s).
   - Tape or other material to affix flip chart sheets to the wall.
   - Large post-it notes
   - Markers: different colours.
   - Optional: small sticky notes or coloured dots for voting.
4. Decide if you want to run this in combination with an PVA or IVA workshop (tool: From PVA to Action).
5. Send out the invitations for your group meeting at least four weeks before your meeting. Communicate Purpose and Objective, when, where and who will be involved. For the CVA:
   - Review the values list template to be used so it is well aligned with the language and words used in your type of business. If your team already has a list of values (espoused values) make sure these values are included in your values list.
   - Decide if the focus of the assessment is going to be on how the team performs, or- on how the team perceives that the organization performs, and model your assessment-questions accordingly.
   - Make sure that you send the team the link to the assessment on time (e.g. 3 weeks) before the workshop.
6. Prepare a presentation together with your trained CTT consultant and identify the key overall outcomes of the assessment. Make sure to include the 7-level model and how to read the tools in the presentation. (In case there's much demographics you will need to decide which overviews are most relevant, e.g. a comparison of current culture outcomes between units, a graphic that compares entropy, etc. You may even include some industry trend numbers; those are available to trained CTT consultants).
7. It helps when the 7-level model is customized to the language and outcomes for this context, where for each of the levels that you present, contains the values that show up in the top 10 outcomes of the CVA. Thus presenting the logic behind the results interpretation early on in your conversation.
8. If needed, print the presentation and/or the CVA results as a handout.
9. Prepare your own answers to the questions that you will ask your audience. Have your own answers to those questions ready as well. We suggest to prepare: "What surprises you?", "What becomes clear to you?", "What stands out as being positive? and "What stands out as being challenging?".
10. It is also good if you prepare the questions you would like to ask the group to further explore and understand the results.
11. Make sure you have practiced the presentation and feel comfortable with the material.
12. If you intend to use a meeting evaluation or team reflection, have it prepared in advance (see page 172).
13. Try to come at least 20 minutes before everyone else.
14. Setup the room with blank flip chart sheets on the walls; well-spaced out so that people can easily read the charts once writing is on them.

15. Be prepared to show the slides.
16. Write the Purpose, Objective and Agenda on a flip-chart so that everyone can see them during the whole session.
17. Make sure you take notes during the meeting or arrange for someone to do so.

DURING THE SESSION

1. Present the Purpose, Objective of the exercise. Highlight when you intend to end the meeting. Ask if everyone will be able to stay for the whole meeting.
2. Introduce the exercise by sharing the steps to be taken (see "Step by Step Instructions" below). Make sure everyone understands the exercise. Allow time for questions and concerns.
3. Explain the importance of understanding the importance of honest and open dialogue, based on respect and trust. Underline that we do this to perform better together in order to reach our strategic objectives and operational results. Remember, the process is as important as the outcome.
4. Conclude the exercise by a reflection followed by what you expect to be the next step on your culture build-up journey.

AFTER THE SESSION

1. Write and send out minutes as soon as possible after the meeting with your agreed key actions and wanted behaviours. Enclose the slides you showed (if requested by any of the participants).
2. How do you intend to reinforce your team's conclusions and make your progress visible? For instance, visual aids, questions, recognition, etc.
3. Now, that you have started to create a shared understanding of expected behaviour, make sure your own personal priorities and behaviour is also aligned, as a leader.
4. How do you intend to follow up the session? A good idea is to plan a team follow-up discussion and also an individual follow-up at your performance review meeting with the participants. See "Culture Report" on page 185, for ideas and tips for continuous follow up and learning.

Agenda / Step by step instructions

A) Presenting the assessment outcomes (2-3 hrs)

1. Connect to your team objectives and long term goals, and describe how this aligns with today's culture assessment. 5–10 min

2. Deliver the Seven Levels of Consciousness presentation and how to read CVA results using a neutral CVA example and explain the indices. This gives the participants an opportunity to see what the plots can show, what the white dots and other unknown items mean. 20 min
For an example presentation check at www.valuescentre.com/getconnected.

3. Put the team results on the screen (and/or as handouts). Let the results speak for themselves. Be prepared to answer questions about the model and tool structure. Avoid sharing your conclusions of what you see at this point. 5–10 min

4. If the group is larger than 6 people, divide them into smaller groups of 3-5 people. Give them 45-60 minutes to discuss and write answers to the following questions on flipcharts you have prepared on the wall: 45–60 min

- What stands out in the results- any surprises, questions?
- What are the positives/strengths? List those.
- What are the challenges or opportunities for development? List those.

Underline that the objective in your conversation is to explore rather than explain; please invite each other to share by asking yourself open questions.

Alternative: Hand out Template 1 to everyone and ask them to first individually reflect and answer, then talk about it to reach a shared meaning within the groups of 3-5 people.

Example:

Template 1:

Reflection on results Team name: *A-Team*

What becomes clear to you?	What is positive?
· *Predictable but "dull"* · *Typical maintanace team* · *Current values are empty on common good levels* · *We want to increase more on internal cohesion (level 5)* · *Very focused on level 3 and 4 at the moment (last 3-4 months)* · *We seem to share information but not co-operate* · *Finance is not an issue*	· *Personal and Desired faily similar and they reflect Volvo IT core values* · *Strong will to move upwards to more of common good* · *We see need for more focus on corp. evolution* · *Few limiting values Low Entrophy (7%)* · *Many choose the same value words in desired resp. current situation*
What can be improved?	**Anything negative?**
· *More of common good* · *Co-operate more* · *Have some fun* · *Limiting value "Caution" - What does it mean?* · *Client Relations could be improved*	· *We have no values on "Client Relations" and "Finance".* · *Corporate evolution has a potentially limiting value*

5. Have a plenary dialogue around all the group's results by reviewing the flipcharts (or templates). Identify the key themes and observations. At the end of the conversation, offer your own insights to those questions. 20 min

6. Next question to be asked: "What do we need to explore further in order to define our next steps?" When needed you may want to vote, determining which of the values you need to focus on for today's session. Document the thoughts on a flipchart. 20 min

7. Agree upon which are the key values to address to perform better together and reach your short- and long term objectives. Conclude with the team what values you would like to explore and work with during the rest of this workshop, and which to address later. 10–20 min

Alternative: Hand out Template 2 and ask everyone to identify which potentially limiting values you need to explore and address to become a low fear team. Let everyone select 1-3 potentially limiting values, depending on how high your overall entropy is. And ask which 2-4 positive values they would like to explore and address to become a high performing team and reach our team objectives. Collect all votes in an anonymous way and display the scores on a flipchart. Have a whole group talk and dialogue about the outcome. Don't only follow the score, but listen to the energy and arguments of the group, before you make your final priority as a group of values to work with. Offer your insights after the discussion is complete.

B) Exploring key values and behaviours for further development (2-3 hrs)

1. Create breakout groups

Depending on group size you determine how many values you would like to focus on. We advise to organize breakout groups with each at least around 3 participants. Make sure that each breakout group has some wall-space and a flipchart (or use Template 3a and 3b).

2. When exploring Potentially Limiting Values 45–60 min

a) The survey identified people's view of what is limiting our ability to succeed. You each have a number of post-it notes. Please write down for the value of your focus: what are the behaviours that we show in the workplace that underline this value? It is important for our leaders to understand how people are experiencing these values or behaviors. Ask the group to please make their comments in complete sentences or clear bullet points on how you see it.
b) Now ask the group to stick the post-its on a flipchart whilst reading them out.
c) After this: ask the group to cluster the behaviours and to then come up with one headline for each of the clusters.
d) Ask the group: in one sentence, how would we define this value for our organization?
e) Then go into the aspect of impact and ask the group: How much does this value impact our day-day work in terms of costs/ effectiveness/ productivity/ motivation etc? Note down on a post-it.

f) Gather post-its on a flipchart: ask the group to prioritize - what is the biggest cost and can this be roughly quantified?

***Alternative:* When exploring Potentially Limiting Values** (using Template 3a) 45–60 min

a) Hand out Template 3a
b) Assign groups of 3-5 people to work with one limiting value at the time.
c) Ask them to individually start to reflect and define their personal view of "Definition" and "Culture" of their selected potentially limiting value.
d) Then ask the group to talk about their individual views and come up with shared "Definition" and "Culture" of their selected potentially limiting value.
e) Based on this outcome, ask the group to brainstorm actions and behaviors that would reduce or eliminate their selected potentially limiting value in our daily operation. Then ask them for each of their identified actions to define if it is ME (each one of us), WE (a team effort) or the COMPANY (structural issue) that has to make this action happen.
f) Then gather all groups and share and discuss your findings and a proposal of actions.

3. When exploring Positive Values 45–60 min

a) The survey has identified Personal, Current or Desired values that will have a positive impact when those are built upon further. In order to create a picture of what this would look like we ask the group to imagine the value .... is now fully adopted by everyone in this team. What are the behaviours that we are seeing us operate by? Ask people to record their thoughts on post-it notes.
b) What does it look and feel like? What are people doing, saying, and feeling? What is different about the place?
c) Once everyone has finished doing this, work as a team to cluster the thoughts into groups and develop a short title to capture the meaning of each cluster
d) Discuss: what is our current position?
   - Score on a scale of 0-10, where 10 is "value is fully present" and 0 is "value is not present".
   - Discuss your team-score, explore why there are differences and try to reach consensus on one score. What behaviours are already carried out? What behaviours do we NOT yet see that would make this a higher score (prioritise). In thinking about behaviours, share real life stories that illustrate these behaviours.

Alternative: **When exploring Positive Values** (using Template 3b) 45–60 min

a) Hand out Template 3b
b) Assign groups of 3-5 people to work with one positive value at the time.
c) Ask them to individually start to reflect and define their personal view of "Definition" and "Culture" of their selected positive value.
d) Then ask them as a group to talk about their individual views and come up with shared "Definition" and "Culture" of their selected positive value..
e) Based on this outcome, ask the group to brainstorm actions and behaviors that would improve and grow the selected positive value in our daily operation. Then ask them for each of their identified action to define if it is ME (each one of us), WE (a team effort) or the COMPANY (structural issue) that has to make this action happen.
f) Then gather all groups and share and discuss your findings and a proposal of actions.

Example:

Template 3b:

Desired value

Team name: *A-Team*

Desired Value	Definition How do WE define this value?	Culture How does this value (behavior) look like when at its best?	Actions to Create What actions can we* take to make this value grow? *) ME personally, WE as a group and the COMPANY/Management?
Cooperation	• *Sharing problems, challenges and opportunities.* • *Take care and support each other.* • *Sharing best practice.* • *Help each others.* • *Sense of joint responsibility and accountability.* • *Propose actions - think forward.* • *Shared vision and long term objectives.* • *Shared values*	• *Unselfish helping someone else to succeed or take on a challenge.* • *1+1=3* • *You don't have to ask for co-operation… it just happens!* • *The joy of sharing a success.* • *Pure and true feeling of "we" - "us".* • *Trust - I know I will get help when I have a challenge or ask for help.* • *Lean, but still possible to free resources.*	• ***WE***: *Have more of common goals. Take active part of defining our shared goals and KPI's.* • ***ME***: *You need to sacrifice your own local/ functional priorities in order to reach our common goals.* • ***COMPANY***: *Create a shared source pool of key resources, maximize our utilization.* • ***ME/WE***: *Improve our internal communication, be open and honest.* • ***ME***: *Bring up and share our success stories and make them visible.*

4. From dialogue to plan

- Ask participants: "Once we get agreement on the values and behaviours, the real journey begins. In leading this, then what are the top three things you as a team can do to solve current bottlenecks and/ or make those aspired values come alive and stay real?"
- Be specific, actionable, and measurable.
- Also ask the group: if you yourself were to take one step in bringing the journey on this value more to life in your workplace: what step would you be prepared to take?
- Note all suggestions; those will form the basis for your Culture Development Plan – Template 4 (See example on page 54).

Example:

Template 4:

Culture Development Plan

Value	Prioritized actions/behaviours	Follow up *(How)*	By When	By Whom	Status

If time allows you, then involve the whole group in identifying the actions and behaviors and put them into your Culture Development Plan. If you run short on time, you could also assign a small group who takes all the proposed actions and works them into a Culture Development Plan. The proposal plan will then be presented to the whole team for comments and approval at a later meeting.

5. Thank everyone.

Explain next steps.
Ask for some fast feedback on how the session went for people
– what worked well and/or what could be improved.

Template 1:

Reflection on results

Team name:

What becomes clear to you?	What is positive?
What can be improved?	**Anything negative?**

HANDOUT

Template 2:

My priority of values to work on — Team name:

Potentially Limiting Values	Desired Values

Template 3a:

Potentially limiting value

Team name:

Potentially Limiting Value	**Definition** How do WE define this value?	**Culture** How does it look like/appear in our daily work situations?	**Preventive actions** What actions can we* take to make this value grow? *) ME personally, WE as a group and the COMPANY / Management?

Template 3b:

Desired value

Team name:

Desired Value	**Definition** How do WE define this value?	**Culture** How does this value (behaviour) look like when at its best?	**Actions to Create** What actions can we* take to make this value grow? *) ME personally, WE as a group and the COMPANY / Management?

Template 4:

Culture Development Plan

Team name:

Value	Prioritized actions/ behaviours	Follow up (How)	By When	By Whom	Status

Optional worksheet for CVA analysis

Based on the results of CVA, complete the following statements:

a. The organization/team has the following matching personal and current culture values:

b. The organization/team has the following matching current and desired culture values:

c. The organization/team identified the following potentially limiting values:

d. The organization/team has a level of cultural entropy of:

e. The most important Value Jumps—the values that employees want to see more of are: These are the values that scored more highly in the Desired Culture than in the Current Culture.

f. Based on the results of this survey we identified the following actions to improve the organization/team's performance:
The goals should be SMART – Specific, Measurable, Agreed, Realistic, Time-Phased.

	Actions	Description	Alignment Goal
No. 1			
No. 2			
No. 3			

What I have learned about the improvements I need to make to improve the values alignment of my organization/team:

VALUES IN ACTION

Session Leader Guide

This workshop is especially designed to help you in a 'wanted values and behaviour' dialogue within your team.

The workshop is useful in all situations of teamwork. It is recommended that you revisit this type of dialogue and discussion with all your stakeholders, for example customer, sponsor, steering committee, partners, suppliers, team members etc.

The workshop focuses on specific common team situations where we leave mental fingerprints behind us depending on the behaviour we choose to use. At a start-up of a team it helps define the expectations and demands. It is also helpful later when the team goes through different phases and is being reshaped for 'follow up', 'reflect', 'recognise' and/or 'fine-tune the defined and wanted behaviours'.

This workshop is built on 4 typical scenarios;

1) group meeting with your team
2) internal team meeting
3) customer meeting
4) upset customer on the phone

You choose scenarios according to your specific situation at the moment in your team. The intention is for you to address the predefined examples of daily situations in these 4 scenarios and decide what is an acceptable and wanted behaviour. You then outline what is unacceptable behaviour in these types of situations, and you should also describe the typical situations expected for your specific team.

PURPOSE
To reflect and discuss behaviours in different day-to-day work situations with your team stakeholders. To align our behaviours with your own, or the customer's espoused core values.

OBJECTIVE
To agree on what is acceptable behaviour and also what is unacceptable behaviour in different day-to-day work situations.
To agree on what we should all do to reinforce acceptable behaviours and what to do if we don't act according to our agreed behaviour.

TIME
The estimated time for this exercise is approx. 2 - 3 hours.

BEFORE THE SESSION

1. Anchor the decision to do the exercise with the group.
2. Read through the whole Session Leader Guide – the best thing is to try out the exercises yourself first so you know the key steps.
3. Book a meeting room. It is best if everyone can sit around a large table in order to put the worksheet in the middle. If your team is large you may use many tables, and if so prepare good mixed groups of 3 - 5 persons
4. Send out the invitation for your group meeting at least two weeks before the meeting. Communicate Purpose and Objective, when, where and who will be involved.
5. Select supporting slides to use at the workshop. Review speaker notes and add your own. There are suggested supporting slides at www.valuescentre.com/getconnected.
6. If you intend to use a meeting evaluation or team reflection, have it prepared in advance (there is a suggested template at page 172)
7. Try to come at least 20 minutes before everyone else.
8. Make sure the meeting room is ready with all the materials needed. Prepare the following material for each groups of 3 - 5 persons:
   - one scissor per table,
   - a set of post-it notes,
   - a flip-chart page,
   - a whiteboard pen
   - a copy of all the selected situations (attached at page 147-150).
   - a form to report the selected 3 - 5 key situations (attached at the end at page 151)
9. Write the Purpose, Objective and Agenda on a flip-chart so that everyone can see them during the whole session.

DURING THE SESSION

1. Start the session by presenting the Purpose, Objective and Agenda of the meeting. Highlight when you intend to end the meeting. Ask if everyone will be able to stay for the whole meeting.
2. Walk the team briefly through your company core values and explain the link to your team and its specific challenges. Explain why we must work with our team culture.
3. Share your thoughts and feelings about this type of work (investment) and the benefits and challenges you may see. Underline why you personally feel/think it is important for us to work with this. Use your emotions to express this.
4. If you have done the exercise with your team earlier, review your progress on "Where you are on your team culture-building journey?" What has been done/ results/ successes? What do you intend to do in the future?
5. Introduce the exercise by reading out the question and steps to be taken by using the agenda slide. Clarify how you intend to use the material after the session. Make sure everyone understands the exercise. Allow time for questions and concerns.
6. Ask each group to prepare their flip-chart paper. Ask them to write espoused company values or team values in a triangle or around a big circle on their flip chart; see an example from Volvo IT Volvo Group below.
7. Then ask them to cut up the cards with the selected day-to-day situations from all four scenarios. One situation only for each card.

Examples:

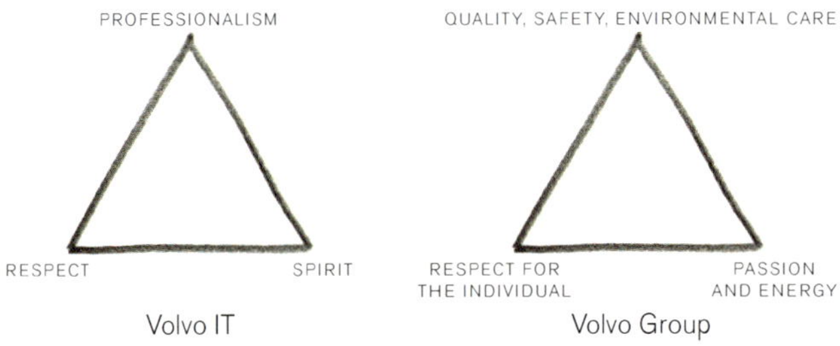

8. Ask the groups to place the cards with the different day-to-day situations relevant to their company or team espoused Core Values on the prepared sheet. It is important that the groups discuss and agree where to put the cards in relation to the Core Values. (See example picture).

9. Now ask the groups to think of any important key situations not mentioned in the predefined situations that they believe should be added. For example, what other day-to-day situations are there in our team where we must have a common behaviour? Ask each person to write down 1 - 3 additional new situations on the post-it notes. One situation only on each post-it.
10. Instruct everyone to place each of their post-it notes with the new key situations in relationship to their espoused Core Values. NB! Ask them to explain to the others what key situation is being added and which Core Values it is most relevant to.

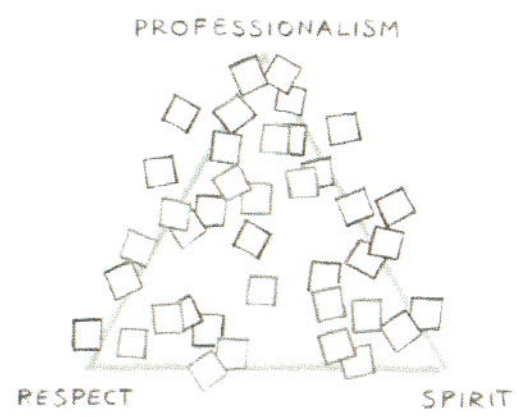

11. From all the situations depicted, each person must select his/her 3 - 5 most important situations where they think we need to have a common behaviour to be able to have a successful team. Then, each group must come to agreement on 3 - 5 prioritised key situations. Mark them clearly and place them on a list on the side. (See picture).

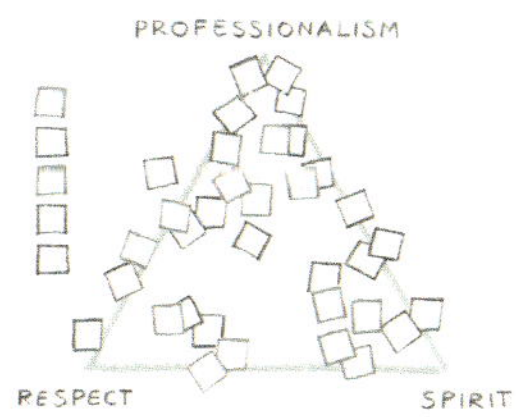

12. Now you have a map of your most important team situations. Lead the team in a discussion to come to an agreement on what should be the WANTED/BEST behaviour and what is UNACCEPTABLE behaviour in each of the selected 3 - 5 key situations. Use the template on page 151.
13. Make sure everyone gets the opportunity to voice his/her view during this phase. Be assertive and probe for questions. Remember, the process is as important as the outcome. Ask the group(s) to write down their conclusions on the template you have handed out (page 151). You will collect these at the end of the workshop.
14. If you have time, use the whiteboard/flipchart to display and align all groups' suggested key situations and defined wanted/best and unacceptable behaviour. The whole team must now select 3–5 situations and behaviours they can agree on as being top priority for your whole team.
15. Conclude the exercise by reading out your final conclusions. Which situations are we already good at? Which situations call for changed behaviour? What should we do to change these behaviours?
16. Clarify agreed upon actions and how we should follow up on our ambitions.

AFTER THE SESSION

1. Write and send out minutes as soon as possible after the meeting with your agreed key situations and wanted/best and unacceptable behaviours. Enclose the slides you showed (if requested by any of the participants).
2. How do you intend to reinforce your team's conclusions and make your progress visible? For instance, visual aids, questions, recognition, etc.
3. Now, that you have started to create a shared understanding of expected norms of behaviour, i.e., "mental fingerprints", make sure your own personal priorities are aligned.
4. How do you intend to follow up the session? A good idea is to plan a team follow-up discussion and also an individual follow-up at your performance review meeting with the participants.

Agenda

(proposal and facilitator notes)

1. Introduction 10 min

Align your team challenges and wanted culture and why it is important to invest in our team culture.

2. Group reflection 5 min

Share your thoughts and feelings about this type of work and the benefits and challenges you see.

3. Work in small groups 60 – 90 min

a. Place the selected team situations in relation to your Core Values on the sheet.
b. What other day-to-day situations are there in our team where we must have a common behaviour? Ask each person to write down their 1 - 3 situations on post-it notes. Instruct the team members to place their post-it notes in relationship to our Core Values on the sheet.
c. Then lead everyone to select the 3 - 5 situations which they agree are the most important for achieving a more competitive and successful team.
d. Once the map is completed, lead the team in a discussion to agree on the wanted/best behaviour and unacceptable behaviour in the selected key situations.

4. Group dialogue 15 – 30 min

Gather the whole group and let the small groups share their results.
Note down comments from the participants.

5. Conclusion and next steps. 10 min

Should we use reflections/feedback to reinforce our learning from this exercise?

HANDOUT

Scenario 1 – Group meeting with your team

People don't appear at meetings and don't inform anyone that they will not participate 1:1	It's difficult to find resources to handle a request from another internal department (I don't have the time…) 1:2	A small request coming from another internal department. The team is in a hectic period and doesn't feel that this is the most important issue to focus on right now. 1:3
That's not my/ our responsibility – "isn't there anyone else who can handle this request….?" 1:4	Offering alternative solutions to the request – be proactive 1:5	Share knowledge and see possibilities in using other departments. 1:6
Us & them. " I've heard they never deliver on time and they cost too much…". 1:7	Recognise good input/ listen to other team members' input and ideas. 1:8	Unclear roles/ decisions - at the end of the meeting 1:9

HANDOUT

Scenario 2 – Internal Team meeting

Bad meeting behaviour – people are not prepared - haven't read the material. 2:1	Handling new customer demands – risks of increasing costs and delays. 2:2	Blaming each other – "you're the weakest link in this team…" 2:3
No updated team charter – what's in the scope? – different views on expectations, scope and time. 2:4	Conflicts within the team – picking on each other. 2:5	Manager wants you to put some more time into another project when you are already fully booked – prioritise. 2:6
Listening to other team members' input. 2:7	Taking the global perspective into consideration – not being close-minded. 2:8	Bad meeting behaviour – people are reading mails, whispering, discussing other things during meetings. 2:9

HANDOUT

Scenario 3 – Customer meeting

The customer doesn't feel we have prioritised him enough. 3:1	Customer questioning our solution – "Is this really the best solution..." 3:2	The customer asks questions you don't understand. 3:3
New/ additional terms from the customer. 3:4	You make promises out of good will that we cannot keep - you are not synchronized towards the customer. 3:5	The customer questions our schedule, another company can do it much faster, to a similar price. 3:6
The customer has heard a rumour that we cannot deliver. 3:7	The customer wants a local solution (and we're a global one). 3:8	The customer wants to know why he should choose your team as a supplier? 3:9

Scenario 4 – Upset customer on the phone

An upset customer calls and you answer – the person responsible is not available and you are about to attend another internal meeting. 4:1	It is not the first time the customer has difficulties in finding the right person. 4:2	The customer is "degrading" my colleagues. 4:3
You are not qualified/competent enough to solve this problem. 4:4	Customer wants to add something that is not in the agreement. 4:5	The customer disagrees with your proposed action – suggests we bend the rules. 4:6
The person I need for an action plan can't be reached due to national holiday. 4:7	You have to do "that little extra" when the conversation is over (it is not just to satisfy – you have to do more). 4:8	

Group:
Date:

Values In Teams Outcome

Priority	Situation	Behaviour	
		Wanted/Best	Unacceptable
1			
2			
3			
4			
5			

NB! Don't forget to agree how we should follow up, like using feedback, reflection, measurements etc.

MY TEAM'S LEVEL OF TRUST

Session Leader Guide

In order to have a high performing team, there must be a high level of trust in the group. Trust increases the speed at which the group is able to accomplish tasks and takes the bureaucracy out of communication. The principal components of trust are character and competence. Trust builds internal cohesion. Trust is the glue that holds people together and the lubricant that allows energy to flow.
The exercise is based on Richard Barretts book "The New Leadership Program".

The Trust Matrix: The principal components of trust are character and competence:

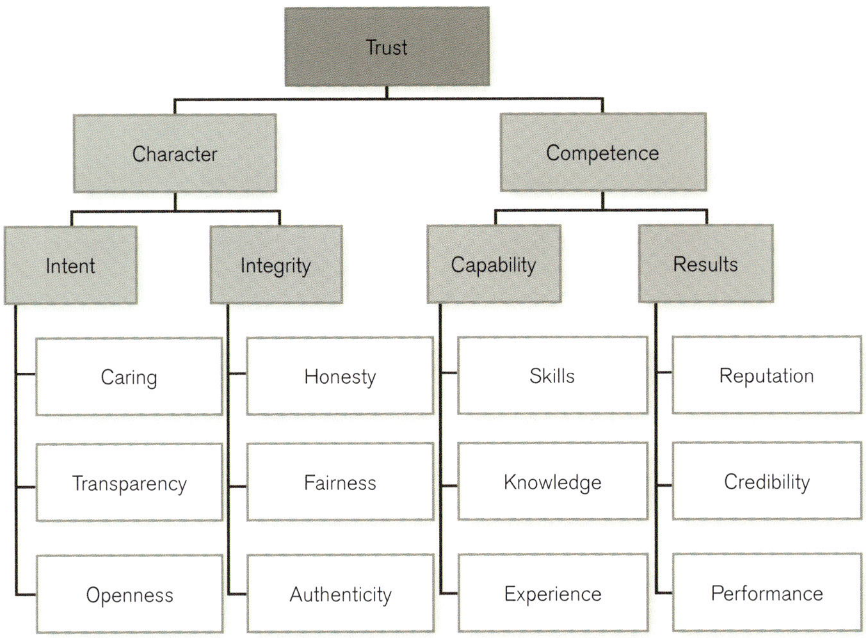

Character is a reflection of how you are on the inside, your intent and the level of integrity you display in your relationship to others. These depend primarily on the level of development of your emotional intelligence and social intelligence. Intent is demonstrated by caring, transparency, and openness; integrity is demonstrated by honesty, fairness and authenticity.

Competence is a reflection of how you are on the outside, your capability and the results you achieve in your role. These depend primarily on the level of development of your mental intelligence, your education and what you have learned during your professional career. Capability is demonstrated by skills, knowledge and experience. Results are demonstrated by reputation, credibility and performance.

PURPOSE
To increase the level of trust in the leadership team.

OBJECTIVE
To identify the strengths and weaknesses of the team with regard to the level of trust they have and make them accountable for improving the situation.

TIME
The estimated time for this exercise is approx. 1 – 2 hours, depending of the size of your team.

BEFORE THE SESSION
1. Anchor the decision to do the exercise in your team.
2. Select participants and book a meeting room.
3. Decide whether you should prepare yourself or use a guest speaker to introduce the workshop and/or create the right atmosphere.
4. Send out an invitation, communicate purpose and objective, when, where and who.
5. Select the slides you intend to use. Look for ideas and select the supporting slides at www.valuescentre.com/getconnected.
6. Make sure the meeting room is ready with all the material needed.
7. If you intend to use a meeting evaluation or reflection, have it prepared in advance (see page 172).
8. Try to come at least 20 minutes before everyone else.
9. Write the Purpose, Objective and Agenda on a flipchart so that everyone can see it during your whole session.

DURING THE SESSION
1. Assemble your team and project The Trust Matrix onto a screen or preferably make two large posters so that everyone can see: one for areas of strength and one for areas of challenge.
2. Present the Purpose, Objective and Agenda of the meeting. Highlight when you intend to end the meeting. Ask if everyone will be able to stay for the whole meeting.
3. Ask the manager to express his/her personal view on how important it is for each participant to clearly understand and articulate their view.
4. Introduce the exercise by sharing the steps to be taken. Make sure everyone understands the exercise. Allow time for questions and concerns.
5. Make sure everyone gets the opportunity to voice his or her view. Be assertive and probe for questions. Remember, the process is as important as the outcome.
6. Conclude the exercise with a shared reflection of the experience and learnings. Ask the question "What have you learned about improving the level of trust in our team"?

AFTER THE SESSION
1. Make sure to follow up and have team reflections on the actions and behaviour that has been identified during the meeting.

Agenda

(proposal and facilitator notes)

1. Introduction 20 min

Go through Purpose, Objective and Agenda.
If needed have an "Ice-breaker" to get everyone connected to each other and the task

Ice-breaker: *Ask everyone to recall a moment in time when they experienced a high level of trust. Who was involved? What was at stake? What made it happen? How did it feel?Finalize the Ice-breaker with a collective reflection of your stories about high trust.*

2. Definition of "trust"? 15 min

Ask the group to define trust. List the key components that come up from the participants on a flipchart or white board so that everyone can read it. Agree on what are the key components.

Ask the group to reflect upon:

Why is trust so important for us?

3. Our level of trust 10 min

Hand out a blank sheet of A4 paper to everyone. Ask everyone to draw a vertical line and grade it from 10 to 1 on their paper (where 10 is high and 1 is low). Ask them to put an "X" on the scale which describes their personal perception of trust in this team. Collect the papers and display all answers on the flipchart.

Ask the group to reflect upon:

What does our picture tell us about our percived level of trust?

4. Trust matrix – strengths and weaknesses 60 min

Step 1: Ask each member of the team to identify which elements of the Trust Matrix they believe are the strongest and weakest in the way the team operates.

Give every person ten points (stick-on dots or marker pen) to allocate to the strengths and ten points to allocate to the challenges. He or she can allocate the points in any combination of each of the twelve components of the trust matrix.

As each person comes forward and mark their points on the two posters —strengths and challenges--they should explain to the rest of the team why they have chosen to allocate the points in that way.

Step 2: When everyone has finished allocating their dots it will become immediately obvious what the strengths and weaknesses are in the way the team operates. Based on the results, begin an open dialogue on how to build on the strengths and minimize the weaknesses that the team has collectively identified.

Step 3: At the end of this dialogue, ask each member of the team to state which elements of the trust matrix he or she is least competent in, and what he or she is doing or can do to improve. Use the Handout at the end of this tool.

This exercise makes the whole team accountable for improving the level of trust.

5. Reflection 15 min

Have the group reflect on the following questions:

- What was the major thing you learned and took away from this meeting?
- What are the success factors to make our agreed actions happen?

HANDOUT

Level of Trust

Trust Matrix Strengths	Trust Matrix Challenges	Proposed Actions to Improve the Level of Trust

THE ELEPHANT IN THE ROOM

Session Leader Guide

The "Elephant in the Room" (in some countries they say "Moose on the Table") is a phrase that means the problems we all know exist but don't have the courage or ability to talk about. These issues or problems get in the way of performance and employee fulfilment and if left unresolved will just get worse and worse.

It is critical that we address these 'undiscussables' in a safe but honest way so that we can shift the negative energy leaks and get back to more productive work and harmonious relationships. In our experience, these sessions will be difficult to start but once the issues are out in the open, people will generally be relieved and have a sense that they can move on.

PURPOSE

To address the problems that are caused by people, process or policy issues that people are unwilling or unable to discuss by themselves.

OBJECTIVE

To increase productivity, quality or employee fulfilment by clearing the negative energy that is getting in the way.

PARTICIPANTS

Ideally, bring the whole team together. If you have to select a smaller group, make sure there is a good cross section of the team members.

TIME

This exercise can take between 2 and 4 hours depending on the size and complexity of the issues that arise. You may have a sense of the issues before the session but be prepared for anything to come up. By definition, these are issues that are below the surface and not being talked about so there may be surprises.

FOR MORE INFORMATION

The Thin Book of Naming Elephants: How to Surface Undiscussables for Greater Organizational Success Sue Annis Hammond (Author), Andrea B. Mayfield (Author)

BEFORE THE SESSION

1. Anchor the decision to do the exercise in your team.
2. Select participants and book a meeting room.
3. Send out an invitation at least two weeks before your meeting. Communicate Purpose and Objective, when, where and who.
4. Make sure the meeting room is ready with all the material needed.
5. If you intend to use a meeting evaluation or reflection, have it prepared in advance (see page 172).
6. Try to come at least 20 minutes before everyone else.
7. Write the Purpose, Objective and Agenda on a flipchart so that everyone can see it during your whole session.

DURING THE SESSION

1. Present the Purpose, Objective and Agenda of the meeting. Highlight when you intend to end the meeting. Ask if everyone will be able to stay for the whole meeting.
2. Ask the manager to express his/her personal view on how important it is for each participant to clearly understand and articulate their personal values as one of the starting points in our values journey.
3. Introduce the exercise by sharing the steps to be taken. Make sure everyone understands the exercise. Recognise that this may be a difficult discussion so set ground rules for honesty and respect. Disagreement is welcomed but only if it is done respectfully. Allow time for questions and concerns.

AFTER THE SESSION

1. How do you intend to reinforce your team's reflections and conclusions (if any), and make your progress visible, that is, visual aids, questions, recognition, etc.?
2. Now that you have started to create a shared understanding of personal values and hot buttons, make sure your behaviour and priorities are aligned e.g. how do we walk our talk?

Agenda

(proposal and facilitator notes)

1. Introduction to the Exercise 15 min

Go through the Purpose, Objectives and Agenda. Be open to questions.

2. Individual reflection and writing 5–10 min

- Pass out 3 index cards/post-it notes to each participant.
- Ask them to write down the top three things the group needs to talk about and isn't (undiscussables). This can be done before the session or during.
- Collect the cards and shuffle to provide some anonymity.
  * See variations 1-3 below

3. Group Prioritisation 15–30 min

- Ask the group to work together to put the cards on a continuum from the most discussable to the least discussable. (You just need a wall and some masking tape.)
- Pick the three "most undiscussable" cards and have the team discuss them one at a time. Let the group pick which they will tackle first.

4. Group Dialogue 1 to 2 hours – take breaks when necessary

- Hold the space for both honesty and respect.
- Encourage exploration of the issue from various perspectives.
- Start to think about possible solutions.

5. Group Reflection 15–20 min

"What is the major benefit that has come from our dialogue?"

Note down the different response on a flip chart with the heading "Connect" as they come up. Verify the responses and note where they are shared and agreed.

- **Variation 1**
  Everybody writes their issue on a card and after a shuffle and redistribution reads the one in their hand as if it were theirs. Even if it is, the discussion is directed at the secret... not the person.
- **Variation 2**
  Before prioritizing and tackling the index cards, ask the participants to list gains and losses for themselves personally and for their work group (or the whole organisation) of not addressing the issues. So for each issue you've got a grid with personal and team gains and losses. This gives a strong visual about how the undiscussable is weighing the organisation down.
- **Variation 3**
  Post the cards during a break and have everyone come in and read all of the posted undiscussables. After a few minutes for participants to absorb the content, the process questions include:
  "what have you learned about our organisation?"
  "what price do we pay for having these undiscussables?" and
  "Are there any of these that should stay undiscussable and why?" Then go into the prioritisation and dialogue.

FROM CONFLICT TO CREATIVITY

Session Leader Guide

There is great strength in diversity. A team comprised of members with different backgrounds, beliefs, world-views, experiences and skills can bring remarkable creativity and results. Sometimes those differences can get in the way and cause conflict which stifles progress and performance. The interpersonal conflicts show up as "counterproductive dialogues" or awkward silences that take up a lot of energy and create toxic work environments. This in turn prevents team members from co-creating the future.

This experience has been designed to unblock our inner capacity to align perspectives and levels of consciousness within our team. It allows us to manage situations with shared vision and common values.

PURPOSE & OBJECTIVE

- To help team members move beyond conflict into creative collaboration.
- To explore the ideas, beliefs and opinions of others without judgement
- To harness the diverse views and beliefs of team members into new creative new solutions

TIME

The estimated time for this exercise is approx. 2 – 3 hours.

BEFORE THE SESSION

1. Anchor the decision to do the exercise with the group.
2. Read through the whole Session Leader Guide – the best thing is to try out the exercises yourself first so you know the key steps.
3. Book a meeting room. Make sure that the room makes it possible to split up the group into pairs and work in pairs in an acceptable way.
4. Send out the invitations for your group meeting at least two weeks before your meeting. Communicate Purpose and Objective, when, where and who will be involved.
5. If you intend to use a meeting evaluation or team reflection, have it prepared in advance (see page 172).
6. Try to come at least 20 minutes before everyone else.
7. Make sure that you have printed hand outs for all participants.
8. Write the Purpose, Objective and Agenda on a flip-chart so that everyone can see them during the whole session.

DURING THE SESSION

1. Present the Purpose, Objective of the exercise. Highlight when you intend to end the meeting. Ask if everyone will be able to stay for the whole meeting.
2. Introduce the exercise by sharing the steps to be taken. Make sure everyone understands the exercise. Optional: Hand out the Seven Level of Consciousness from page 197. Allow time for questions and concerns.
3. Explain the strengths and possible pitfalls of team diversity. Use the Seven Levels Model to show that different people may see situations and challenges differently depending on their values, beliefs and world views. E.g. people who are strongly

focused on level 2 will want to create a sense of belonging, inclusion and harmony but may get stuck in consensus. People who are strongly focused at level 3 want to create efficiency, order and excellence but they may forget to create a shared vision where team members feel aligned and committed.

4. Sensitively ensure that everyone gets the opportunity to voice his or her insights and learning from this exercise. Remember, the process is as important as the outcome.
5. Conclude the exercise with a reflection followed by what you expect to be the next step on your culture build-up journey.

AFTER THE SESSION

1. How do you intend to reinforce your team's reflections and conclusions (if any), and make your progress visible, that is, visual aids, questions, recognition, etc.?
2. How will team members support each other in taking the next steps or actions they have identified?

Agenda

(proposal and facilitator notes)

1. Introduction to the Exercise 10 min

Go through Purpose, Objective and Agenda. Be open for questions.

2. Individual work and reflection 20 -30 min

Ask the participants to complete the hand out and work through the steps in the exercise individually. This is personal reflection time.

3. Role plays 30 -45 min

Form pairs and ask the participants to share their stories and insights.

4. Whole Group Reflection 30 min

Have the group reflect on what was the major thing they learned and took away from this exercise.

Process for understanding and planning your action

1. Select a difficult working situation (involving real team members) that you wish to transform "right after" this experience.

2. Describe the unsatisfactory response that you have currently received from your colleagues or team member partners: e.g.
   - What are they in denial about…
   - What have they shown much resistance to…
   - What have they agreed to, but things are not moving forward as they should...

3. Describe what you wish to happen or what you want to achieve with the team: e.g.
   - I want them to commit to…
   - I want them to fulfil what they have promised, in relation to …
   - I want to see accountability…

4. Remember the contents of your last conversation with these people, about the issues mentioned in steps 2 and 3.

5. Write the dialogue and the impact of the conversation on performance. Also write about their answers when deadlines or requirements had not been met.

6. Albert Einstein famously wrote that "Problems cannot be solved in the same level of consciousness they has been created". To transform this situation or relationship, you must understand the conflict between the Levels of Consciousness that you and those you are in conflict with are currently using in these conversations.

7. Use the Seven Level of Consciousness Diagram on page 197 to identify:
   - The current Levels of consciousness (ideas, thinking, solutions) that are causing the conflicts or blocks.
   - The required Levels of consciousness that will enable you to co-create the solution or path forward.

8. Once you have your "Action Plan", we recommend a Role Play to practice the use of new Levels of Consciousness.

Instructions for the development of the Role Playing Experience

Role A: You will represent the other person (the person you are in disagreement or conflict with)
Role B: One of your colleagues will represent you (using your plan and the protocol)
Role C: The third colleague will be the observer (giving feedback to participant "a" and changing roles with participant "b" every five minutes)

Role Play Steps	Role
1. Create a positive, not threatening, "win – win" atmosphere; the objective is building trust driven commitment.	*All*
2. Give positive feedback to your team member partner, on real working and management issues significant for this person.	*B and C*
3. Communicate the objective of the conversation, in a direct and clear way. Use specific and short statements, to describe one matter at a time.	*All*
4. Actively listen to their responses, without judging them, identify from which of Seven Levels of Consciousness they reason and argue. the Levels of Consciousness.	*B*
5. Use open questions to identify "how and from where" they perceive the barriers preventing the achievement of the results you want to achieve.	*B*
6. Paraphrase the answers, to check/recognise the positive intention of their current levels of Consciousness by stating: "I can see what you're interested in …" "I appreciate your concern about... in order to…"	*B*
7. Communicate the intention of your requirements, by declaring the benefits at the level of awareness of your colleague.	*A*
8. Reconcile the maps, integrating benefits from the perspectives of people involved in implementation.	*A and B*
9. Check your team member's comprehension of the "win-win-win" benefits of implementing the new collaborative plan.	*A*
10. Come to an agreement on how and when to implement the requirements; if you come across more problems, restart this process again from step 4.	*All*
11. Close the conversation, celebrating the agreement and expressing your confidence in a timely implementation.	*All*

Reflection on your findings in this experience:

What have I discovered during this experience?

What have I realized?

Which is my commitment?

How can I make the best use of this technique in my work?

TEAM LEARNING

Session Leader Guide

We all have individual preferences on how we learn best. Some learn best when they plan what to do, while some benefit most from doing. Others learn best from reflecting on what has already been done and then there are those who are at their best when they can connect with others and devise a mutual purpose.

What we all have in common is that as adults we need time and space to debrief and reflect on what we have done in order to augment our earlier beliefs and ingrained principles with new beliefs and values. Often we feel that we have no time for reflection and learning. However, team learning helps each individual envision their self in the change curve, reduce the time it takes to transform and learn and thus enhance the group's ability.

Flexible action and ability to learn collectively is crucial for survival and success in an environment of faster change, and that calls for transformation of our behaviour!

This exercise is built on three main blocks, where the recommendation is to use the first two blocks initially, while the last block could be run on a regular basis. The blocks are:

1. The Prerequisites for Our Learning
2. Team Learning Wheel and Our Learning Styles
3. Team Reflection

This exercise is based upon "The Fifth Discipline Fieldbook: Strategies and Tools for Building a Learning Organization" by Senge, P., Roberts, C., Ross, R., Smith, B., and Kleiner, A.

PURPOSE

To collectively enhance your team's ability to transform and learn as you move through the team's life cycle.

OBJECTIVE

At the end of the exercise everyone should be able to learn from what is happening here and now. Then move beyond their own comfort zones and challenge and make real value shifts.

TIME

This varies considerably. Sometimes a short 10-minute reflection gives a lot, while in other cases an entire day or two will be insufficient.
The most important thing here is to create a language and a way of working with your team to achieve team reflection. The team will need time and repetition to include in their shared culture the process of how they learn together.
Time allocation must come from you as the leader – you need to prioritise and give them the go-ahead to use time for reflection.

BEFORE THE SESSION

1. Anchor the decision to do the exercise with the group.
2. Read through the whole Session Leader Guide – the best thing is to try out the exercises yourself first so you know the key steps.
3. Book a meeting room where it is possible to work in pairs in an acceptable way.
4. Send out the invitation for your group meeting at least two weeks before your meeting. Communicate Purpose and Objective, when, where and who will be involved.
5. Select supporting slides to use at the workshop. Review speaker notes and add your own. You can find suggested slides at www.valuescentre.com/getconnected.
6. Try to come at least 20 minutes before everyone else.
7. Write the Purpose, Objective and Agenda on a flip-chart so that everyone can see them during the whole session.

DURING THE SESSION

1. Follow the proposed agenda.

Block 1: The Prerequisites for Our Learning

2. Ask the participants to individually reflect on the topic:
"Think of a time in your life when you learned more in a short time than any other time. Describe the situation, your thoughts and feelings"
3. Divide the group into pairs and let them share their reflections.
4. Gather the group again for a whole group reflection on the question:
"What were the prerequisites that made your learning experience so effective?"

Block 2: Team Learning Wheel and Our Learning Styles

5. Draw up the figure described below on a whiteboard or flip chart. Start by asking everyone to draw the same two axes and labels on a piece of paper. ① Ask them to first judge themselves if they are "More Concrete" or "More Abstract" as a person. Mark with an "X" where they feel it best describes themselves. ② Then ask the same regarding "More Action" or "More Reflection"? Mark with another "X" then draw an horizontal and a vertical line from the two x:es. ③ And make a big "X" in the graph as shown below.

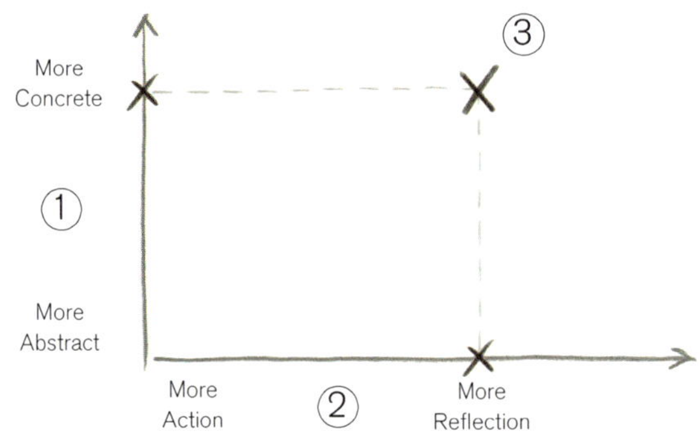

6. Ask each one of the participants to come up and plot their "X"..
   The outcome for the whole group could look similar to the example below.

7. Find the centre point at each axis and draw one vertical and one horizontal line from these centre points, as in the figure below.

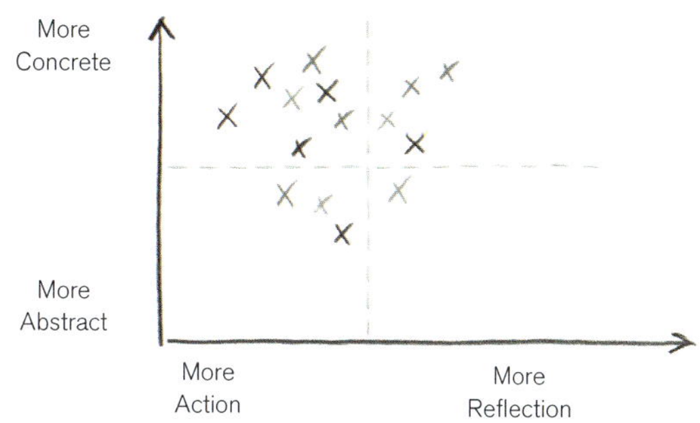

8. Show and introduce the slide below and let the group reflect on the questions:
   - "What does it say about the group learning style?"
   - "Which are our strengths?"
   - "Which steps do we go through in our daily work? Do we take the shortcut (the dotted gray arrow) or do we take time for Public reflection and Shared meaning?"

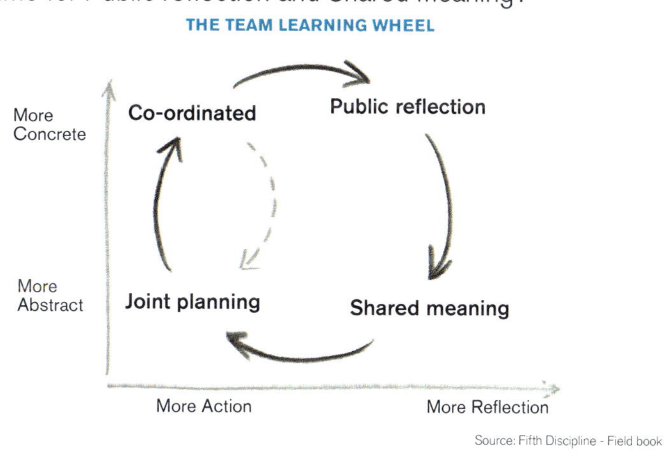

Block 3: Team Reflection

9. Emphasise the difference between discussion and dialogue (See p. 22). Discussion is based on right and wrong statements whereas dialogue is based on the belief that there is no right and wrong. Good reflection is based on dialogue and fearless statements about what each team member has experienced in terms of feelings, thoughts and learning. A good dialogue emerges easier when "we agree that we don't have to agree".

10. Write on a flipchart what you want the group to reflect on. Choose a situation, an experience or find your own topic or select one from the attached example; "Possible reflective questions" at page 170-171. Encourage clarification and adjustments to what you have written. Try to be specific in time and scope.
11. Ask everyone to work individually for 5 - 7 minutes writing down their own feelings, thoughts and learning about the selected situation or topic.
12. Invite them to start sharing. Encourage and give recognition to everyone who is sharing, especially in the beginning and during the first reflections, in order to diminish fear and build trust in the process. Work with Listening, Voicing, Respecting and Suspending. Focus on exploring and explaining. Don't steer or judge. Trust the process. Welcome whatever emerges.

Wrap up

13. Have a team reflection of what insights the exercise has given, and how it might impact own mindset and ambitions to strengthen skills (look at the attached reflection questions; "Team Follow up & Reflection" on page 172).
Write down the team reflections on a whiteboard/flip chart so that everyone can see and build on each other's reflections.
14. Let the team conclude what they find as critical for them in order to get a more fruitful learning climate.
15. Ask if everyone can agree to set aside more time for Reflection in their daily work and at meetings. Try also to come to an agreement on how to follow up the agreed intentions.

AFTER THE SESSION

1. Write and send out minutes as soon as possible after the meeting. Enclose the slides you showed (if requested by any of the participants).
2. How do you intend to follow up the session? A good idea is to plan a follow up dialogue.
3. Plan for your next reflection, not too far away in time.

Agenda

(proposal and facilitator notes)

1. Introduction 10 min

Go through Purpose, Objective and Agenda. Be open to questions.

Block 1 (Optional)

2. The Prerequisites for Our Learning 20 – 30 min

Ask the participants to individually reflect on their personal learning experiences. Let them share their reflections in pairs.

3. Group dialogue 10 – 20 min

Let the whole group share and reflect on what were the prerequisites that made their learning experience effective.

Block 2 (Optional)

4. Team Learning Wheel and Our Learning Styles 10 min

Ask everyone to individually reflect on their personal learning style related to the diagram on the flip chart according to the instructions.

5. Group Dialogue 10 – 20 min

Let all the participants try to plot what they regard as where their learning style best fits and continue the exercise according to the instructions. Reflect on the outcome. What do we learn from this picture?

Block 3

6. Team Reflection 20 – 60 min

Note down a topic or use "Open Space" (see page 66) and let the group choose the topic they find most important to reflect upon at this meeting. Let the participants start with individual reflection (5 minutes) and thereafter start to share their reflections in the group. Note down the reflections on a flip chart, so everyone can see them. Remember: The purpose is the reflection, not to reach conclusions.

Wrap up

7. Evaluation of the exercise 20 – 30 min

Have the group reflect on what was the major thing they learned and took away from this exercise and try to agree on how to improve the Team Learning ability in the team.

HANDOUT

Possible reflective questions:

1. Describe a situation where our team really made a difference for ME!

2. Name two things we really need to start doing, in order to use time more effectively.

3. Name two things we really need to stop doing!

4. What's the glue that keeps us together in our team?

5. How can we see and measure progress?

6. What am I really passionate about?

Source: PREERA Consulting

7. What would it take for us to go to the "next level of development" in our team collaboration?

8. What would it take for us to resolve dilemmas with guidance of our vision?

9. What drives me in my life today?

10. What do I need to focus on to create what I think is attainable?

11. What do I think WE need to focus on in order to attain what is possible?

12. What really influences me?

HANDOUT

Team Follow-up & Reflection:

1. What is the most important thing you've learnt during the workshop?

2. Rate your overall impression of the exercise on a scale of 1 - 5 (5=high). Complement your rating with a short comment.

3. What suggestions for improvement do you see for this workshop?

4. What are your expectations for the next step after this workshop?

5. Other comments

EFFECTIVE FEEDBACK

Session Leader Guide

This exercise helps the team members to be proactive in creating a positive feedback atmosphere within the team that will reinforce, encourage and motivate the team members when facing different types of challenges.

Effective feedback should enable a receiver to walk away understanding exactly what he or she did and what impact it had on them. When the result is this specific and this direct, there is a better chance that the person getting the feedback will be motivated to begin, continue or stop behaviours that affect performance. (Sloan R. Weitzel: "Feedback that works")

This exercise has its focus on the SBI Feedback Model and is based upon "Ongoing Feedback: How to Get It, How to Use It – An Ideas into Action Guidebook" issued by Centre for Creative Leadership.

Many different surveys have shown that positive and accurate feedback is one of the top enhancers of performance. There is also an alternative to this exercise named "Whale Done!" which consists of a book, a DVD and exercise material. This practice has a stronger focus on the positive and how to avoid negative criticism and instead use 'redirective' and 'reinforcing' positive feedback.

'Whale Done' will help your employees learn how to build trust, accentuate the positive, and when a mistake occurs, redirect the energy for a more productive outcome. It provides a clear, easy-to-use approach that will help employees discover the power of positive relationships and enable them to make more effective choices in their interactions with co-workers. (2002, VisionPoint Productions and The Ken Blanchard Companies)

PURPOSE

To collectively enhance your team's ability to use positive and redirecting feedback as a way to strengthen the team spirit.

OBJECTIVE

At the end of the exercise everyone should be aware of how their way of giving and receiving feedback can have an impact on both the motivation and performance of their colleagues.
A recommendation is to conclude the exercise with an agreement that everyone will strive to apply these skills in their daily interactions.

TIME

Estimated time for this exercise is approx. 1 – 2 hours.

BEFORE THE SESSION

1. Anchor the decision to do the exercise with the group.
2. Read through the whole Session Leader Guide – the best thing is to try out the exercises yourself first so you know the key steps.
3. Book a meeting room that makes it possible to work in pairs in an acceptable way.
4. Send out the invitation for your group meeting at least two weeks before your meeting. Communicate Purpose and Objective, when, where and who will be involved. Attach to the invitation a description of the SBI Model that is attached at the end of this tool (pages 176-178) and ask them to read through and reflect on their own way of managing feedback.
5. Select supporting slides to use at the workshop. Review speaker notes and add your own. You will find supporting slides at www.valuescentre.com/getconnected. Here you can download the pocket cards, which you can print and hand out as reinforcement material.
6. If you intend to use a meeting evaluation or team reflection, have it prepared in advance.
7. Try to come at least 20 minutes before everyone else.
8. Write the Purpose, Objective and Agenda on a flip-chart so that everyone can see them during the whole session.

DURING THE SESSION

1. Follow the proposed agenda on page 175.
2. Gather the group again for a whole-group reflection.
3. Have a team reflection of which insights the exercise has given, how it might impact their own feedback skills and their ambitions to strengthen them (look at suggested reflection questions in the exercise Team Learning; "Team Follow up & Reflection" on page 172).
   Write down the team reflections on a whiteboard/flip chart so that everyone can see and build on each other's reflections.
4. Let the team conclude what they find as critical for them in order to get a more open and positive feedback climate.
5. Ask if everyone can agree to apply the feedback guidelines in their daily work and interactions. Try also to come to an agreement of how to follow up the agreed intentions e.g. by planning a follow-up meeting, as part of the individual performance reviews, appraisal discussions, etc.
6. Distribute, if available, the pocket cards and promote the use of them as a reminder of the importance of accurate and positive feedback.

AFTER THE SESSION

1. Write and send out minutes as soon as possible after the meeting. Enclose the slides you showed (if requested by any of the participants).
2. Make sure you follow up on your agreement and note what you have learnt from your progress of the work with effective feedback. NB! Especially important is that you as a leader "walk the talk" and lead the way to work actively with feedback. Acknowledge people doing things right, when you see them give each other feedback.
3. Build in feedback as a normal way of operating in your daily work.

Agenda
(proposal and facilitator notes)

1. Introduction 10 min

Go through Purpose, Objective and Agenda. Be open to questions.

2. Reflection in small groups 10 – 30 min

Ask the participants to select a partner and share their reflections/conclusions/concerns regarding feedback on the hand out (page 176-178), that they have read prior to the meeting.

3. Group dialogue 30 – 60 min

Make a presentation of the meaning and benefits of effective feedback. Let the group reflect over what has been presented and share their opinions of what they would like to bring to the team.

4. Agree 10 – 30 min

Based on your reflections and learnings what are your shared meanings? Have the team agree to follow the basic principles outlined on the feedback pocket card.

5. Reflection 10 – 20 min

Have the group reflect on what was the major thing they learned and took away from this exercise.

The SBI Feedback model

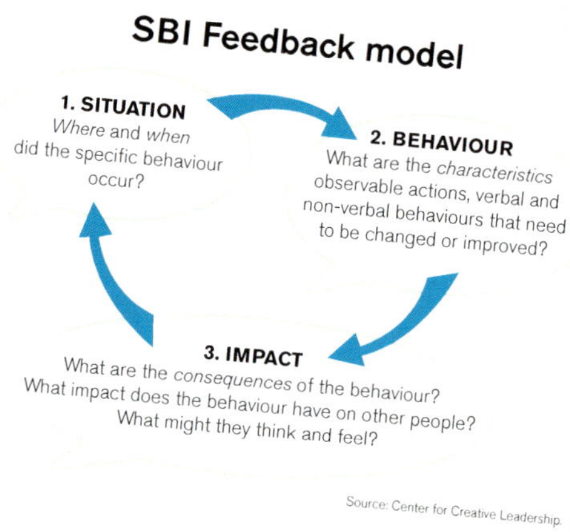

Feedback lets us know how we are doing. It can be used in our everyday work to see if we are meeting expectations. If you have set a developmental goal, it reinforces the changes you are making – it encourages you to continue. If you are in a new job, it will help you understand whether you are learning the new skills that are required.

We must, however, be proactive in creating a positive feedback atmosphere. It is one part of our culture journey.

We recommend the use of the Centre for Creative Leadership's "SBI Model" (Situation, Behaviour, Impact). The model:

- Provides a framework for structuring information.
- Helps us provide feedback which is specific and helpful.
- Is a safe way to give feedback.

The model is very simple and thus easy to remember and use. To give feedback this way, you describe the situation where the behaviour occurred, then you describe the behaviour that you observed, and finally you describe the impact the behaviour had on you or the group.

- **Situation:** Where and when did the specific behaviour occur?
  "During our meeting today when we were discussing the financial aspects of our new project…"

- **Behaviour:** What are the characteristics, observable actions, verbal and non-verbal behaviours that need to be changed or improved?
  "You interrupted me several times…"

- **Impact:** What are the consequences of the behaviour? What impact does it have on other people? Is the behaviour effective? Ineffective?
  "It made me feel that you were not interested in what I was saying. It made me feel as if you did not appreciate the contribution I was trying to make. I think this strongly impacted the group's decision-making process because they missed some strategic information."

Do's and Don'ts for Receiving Feedback

Do

- Let the person finish what she/he is saying
- Ask clarifying questions
- Ask for specifics if not provided
- Pay attention to your nonverbal responses
- Ask the person to give you alternatives to your behaviour
- Respect those who do not wish to give you feedback
- Thank the person for being helpful to you

Don't

- Become defensive or explain your behaviour
- Interrupt the other person
- Be afraid of silence or pauses
- Ask the person to defend his/her opinion
- Seek feedback from those who you know will only give you positive reinforcement

Evaluate the Feedback

- **Accuracy:** Who is giving the feedback? What are their intentions? How much do you respect their opinion?

- **Value:** Does the feedback have meaning to you or not? Is it something that can be helpful to you? Do you want to know more?

- **Importance:** What are you going to do about it?

Source: Centre for Creative Leadership. Ongoing Feedback: How to Get It, How to Use It – An Ideas into Action Guidebook. www.ccl.org

HANDOUT

Questions for reflection of own feedback skills.

1. How often do you give feedback to your colleagues and others?

2. What is normally the reason for your feedback? Performance, attitudes, behaviours, looks?

3. What type of feedback do you most often provide? Positive, negative, redirecting?

4. What holds you back i.e. prevents you from giving feedback more often?

5. How does it feel when you receive feedback yourself? How do you want it to be given to you?

SKILFUL DISCUSSION

Session Leader Guide

This exercise helps a team to make their thought processes transparent, to bring assumptions to the surface and perhaps challenge them. Also, to look more closely at sources of disagreement.

This exercise is based upon "The Fifth Discipline Fieldbook: Strategies and Tools for Building a Learning Organization" by Senge, P., Roberts, C., Ross, R., Smith, B., and Kleiner, A.

PURPOSE

To collectively enhance your team's awareness of the impact of Skilful Discussions on daily performance.

OBJECTIVE

At the end of the exercise everyone should be aware of what impact their behaviour in a discussion could have on the outcome and how to achieve a better result.
A recommendation is to conclude with an agreement that everyone will strive to apply these skills in future meetings.

TIME

Estimated time for this exercise is approx. 1 - 2 hours.

BEFORE THE SESSION

1. Anchor the decision to do the exercise with the group.
2. Read through the whole Session Leader Guide – the best thing is to try out the exercises yourself first so you know the key steps.
3. Book a meeting room that makes it possible to work in pairs in an acceptable way.
4. Send out the invitation for your group meeting at least two weeks before your meeting. Communicate Purpose and Objective, when, where and who will be involved. Attach to the invitation a description of what we mean by a 'Skilful Discussion' (attached at the end of this document, page 182-184) and ask them to read it through and reflect on their own experiences.
5. Select supporting slides to use at the workshop. Review speaker notes and add your own. You will find suggested slides at www.valuescentre.com/getconnected. Here, you can also download suggested pocket cards, which you can print and use as reinforcement material.
6. If you intend to use a meeting evaluation or team reflection, have it prepared in advance (see page 172).
7. Try to come at least 20 minutes before everyone else.
8. Write the Purpose, Objective and Agenda on a flip-chart so that everyone can see them during the whole session.

DURING THE SESSION

1. Follow the proposed agenda on page 181.
2. Divide the group into pairs and let them share their reflections/conclusions/concerns with their partner.
3. Gather the group again for a whole group reflection.
4. Have a team reflection of what insights the exercise has given, how it might impact their own mindset and ambitions to strengthen their skills (look at the suggested reflection questions in the exercises 'Team Learning'; "Team Follow up & Reflection"). Write down the team reflections on a whiteboard/flip chart so that everyone can see and build on each other's reflections.
5. Let the team conclude what they consider critical for them in order to get a more fruitful discussion climate.
6. Ask if everyone can agree to apply these guidelines in their daily work and meetings. Try also to come to an agreement of how to follow up the agreed intentions e.g. by planning a follow-up meeting as part of the individual performance reviews, appraisal discussion, etc.
7. Distribute, if available, the pocket cards and promote the use of them as a reminder of the importance of skilful discussions.

AFTER THE SESSION

1. Write and send out minutes as soon as possible after the meeting. Enclose the slides you showed (if requested by any of the participants).
2. Make sure you follow up on your agreement and note what you have learnt from your progress of the work with skilful discussions.
3. Have a follow up reflection about your discussion climate within 2 - 4 weeks to make sure you all start to practice and live by your skilful discussion agreement. Make adjustment in agreement, if needed.

Agenda
(proposal and facilitator notes)

1. Introduction 10 min

Go through Purpose, Objective and Agenda. Be open for questions.

2. Reflection in small groups 10 – 30 min

Ask the participants to select a partner and share their reflections/ conclusions/concerns on the handout "What is Skilful Discussion?" (page 182-184).

3. Group dialogue 30 – 60 min

Make a presentation of the meaning and benefits of 'Skilful Discussion'. Let the group reflect on what has been presented and ask them to share their opinions of what they would like to bring to the team.

4. Reflection 10 – 20 min

Have the group reflect on what was the major thing they learned and took away from this exercise.

What is a Skilful Discussion?

In skilful discussion, the team intends to come to closure, in order to make a decision, reach agreement, or identify priorities. Skilful discussion incorporates some of the techniques of action learning and dialogue, but it is always focused on a real task at hand. It helps a team learn to make their thought processes transparent, to bring to the surface and challenge assumptions, and to look more closely at sources of disagreement.

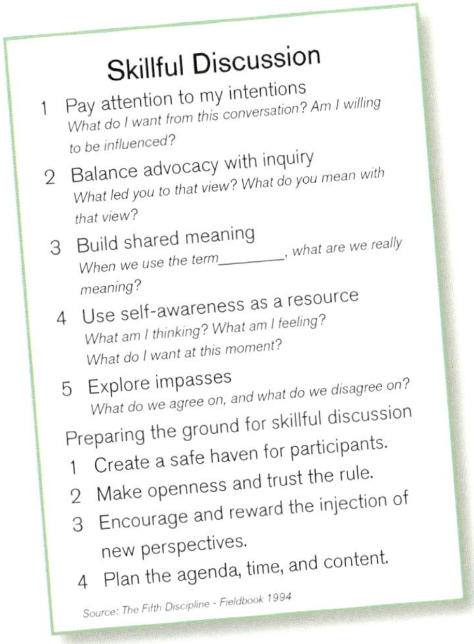

Skillful Discussion

1 Pay attention to my intentions
What do I want from this conversation? Am I willing to be influenced?

2 Balance advocacy with inquiry
What led you to that view? What do you mean with that view?

3 Build shared meaning
When we use the term________, what are we really meaning?

4 Use self-awareness as a resource
What am I thinking? What am I feeling? What do I want at this moment?

5 Explore impasses
What do we agree on, and what do we disagree on?

Preparing the ground for skillful discussion

1 Create a safe haven for participants.

2 Make openness and trust the rule.

3 Encourage and reward the injection of new perspectives.

4 Plan the agenda, time, and content.

Source: The Fifth Discipline - Fieldbook 1994

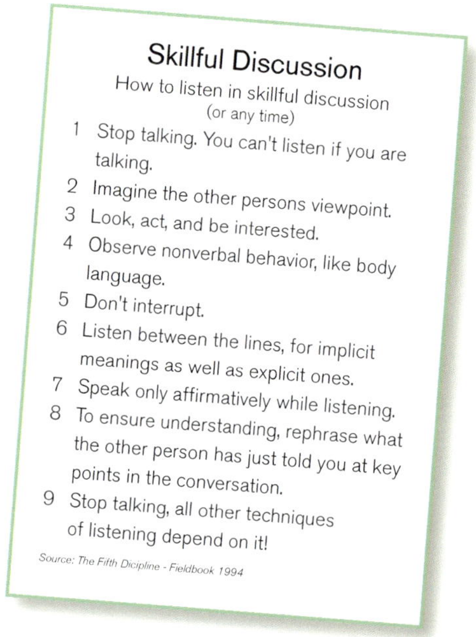

Skillful Discussion

How to listen in skillful discussion
(or any time)

1 Stop talking. You can't listen if you are talking.

2 Imagine the other persons viewpoint.

3 Look, act, and be interested.

4 Observe nonverbal behavior, like body language.

5 Don't interrupt.

6 Listen between the lines, for implicit meanings as well as explicit ones.

7 Speak only affirmatively while listening.

8 To ensure understanding, rephrase what the other person has just told you at key points in the conversation.

9 Stop talking, all other techniques of listening depend on it!

Source: The Fifth Dicipline - Fieldbook 1994

The most important part of skilful discussion is the commitment team members make to follow the five protocols.

1. **Pay attention to your intentions.** It is important that each team member understands what she/he wants to accomplish in the discussion. If you are not willing to be influenced, what is the purpose of the conversation? Be clear on what you want and do not mislead others as to your intentions.
2. **Balance advocacy with inquiry.** If this is not done, the team will just sit and listen to each other's position statements. People's assumptions will not even surface, much less be challenged. In this case what people are really thinking will surface in the hallway after the meeting.
3. **Build shared meaning.** If people understood that words are symbols and have different meanings to different people, then everyone would routinely check what others mean and there would be far less miscommunication. If you want to create shared meaning it is very important to use language with precision and to question what is really meant – what is the meaning behind the words? As you talk around the meaning, you will get closer to a precise definition, which everyone can agree on.
4. **Use self-awareness as a resource.** When you are feeling confused, angry, frustrated, concerned, or troubled in a meeting, ask yourself the following questions:
   a. **What am I thinking?** (pause)
   b. **What am I feeling?** (pause)
   c. **What do I want at this moment?** (pause)

You will often end up with insights about the team's assumptions or your own concerns, which you can then discuss with the team.

5. **Explore impasses.** When the team seems to be "running into a brick wall", ask, "What do we agree on, and what do we disagree on?" "Can we pinpoint the source of our disagreement?" Often sources of disagreement fall into one of four categories.
   a. **Facts** – What exactly has happened? What is the "data"?
   b. **Methods** – How should we do what we need to do?
   c. **Goals** – What is our objective?
   d. **Values** – Why do we think it must be done in a particular way? What do we believe in?

   Simply agreeing on the source of disagreement often allows people to learn more about the situation, clarify assumptions, and then move forward.

   Three things might help the team when this happens.
   a. Listen to ideas as if for the first time. Work at being open to new ideas.
   b. Consider each person's "mental model" as a piece of a larger puzzle. Look at the issues from the other person's perspective.
   c. Ask yourself (and everyone else): 'What do we need to do to move forward?'

The Skilful Discussion pocket card also lists nine ways to improve listening in skilful discussion (or any time)!

Source: Senge, P., Roberts, C., Ross, R., Smith, B., and Kleiner, A. (1994).
The Fifth Discipline Fieldbook: Strategies and Tools for Building a Learning Organization.

Questions for reflection of own experiences

1. *What has dominated the meetings you have taken part in during the last month? Debate, Discussion or Dialogue? What impact has the discussion climate had on your team performance and result?*

2. *Recall a situation when you left a meeting saying to yourself "This was a good and constructive meeting".*
   - *What was the situation?*
   - *What was at stake?*
   - *How were you involved?*
   - *What made this meeting so successful?*

CULTURE REPORT

Session Leader Guide

Culture is something intangible and subjective that at first instance could be regarded as difficult to measure in an objective and tangible way. But it helps if we view culture for what it is, something that is growing and developing through dialogue and learning, and avoid the mindset that every measurement has to be rational and numerical. Additionally we need to have ways to recognise and follow up on progress during our journey to grow our wanted culture. This tool provides the potential.

It is based on the collective dialogues and actions that we have done in order to grow our wanted culture during the last 2 - 3 months. The process of developing the report brings to the surface what we have discovered and learned from these actions and dialogues. It also highlights the insights and conclusions that we have reached when analysing the different types of measurements we have done during the last few months. Like what perspectives and conclusions we have reached from engagement surveys, values assessments, customer satisfaction surveys, etc. It also includes our conclusions about whether our wanted culture is growing in the strategic and desired direction or not, and what we intend to do in order to continue to take care of and/or improve our culture.

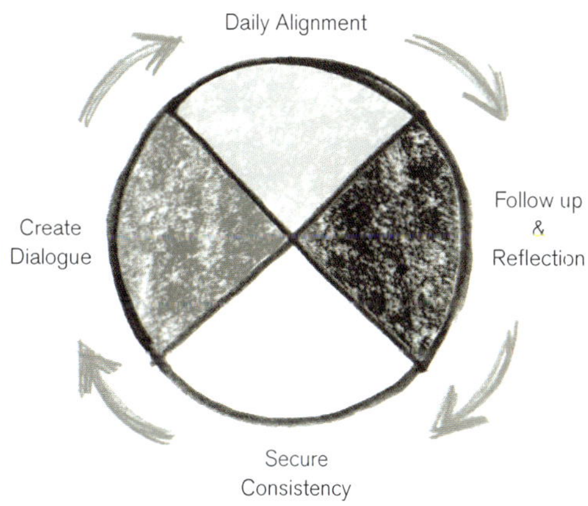

The approach in this tool is actually a team learning exercise built on Kolb's learning wheel, with aligned questions regarding our culture journey. The tool is primarily aimed at managers and leaders who lead the cultural transformation in a team or organisation.

PURPOSE

To create a shared picture of the status of our current culture journey, through data collection and dialogue.

OBJECTIVE

A written two page report displaying our culture, which we can communicate to our steering group/board and to our employees.
The Culture Report consists of:

- actions
- measurements and reflections
- strategic alignments
- corrective actions/tools

The approach below describes how you and your team can create routines to describe your culture development on a quarterly basis. As distinct from traditional reports it also offers you and your team a way to recognise and learn from your development, not only reporting your status.

STARTING UP THE PROCESS

1. Anchor the decision to work with quarterly Culture Reports in your Management Team, and agree with your Steering Committee or Board what this will look like and why and how it will be done.
2. Define who should be in charge of the making and driving of the Culture Report, plus who should be involved. The report must be owned by the manager of the team or unit, and shall be a natural part of the standing agenda for follow up on performance.
   It is recommended that you start by having your Managing Team create your report during the first year in order to understand what it is, and what value it will bring before you delegate the task to someone else.
3. Make sure that "Culture Report" is part of your next performance review meeting. Set aside at least 1 - 2 hours.
4. In preparing for the meeting, make sure you select what actions have been done during the last period, answering the following questions in the different parts of the report:

For the "Create Dialogue" section

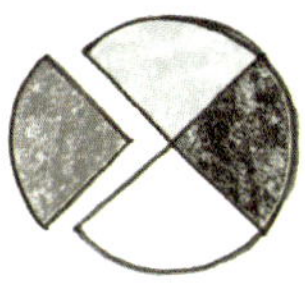

- What has been done to create and develop your ability to have focused dialogues around your wanted culture, like our vision, mission and values? It could be development activities like training workshops, reinforcement material, and so on that stimulates and enables us to talk and connect.
- What changes have you made in your "social structure" to make it easier for everyone to behave and act according to your wanted culture and values?

For the "Daily Alignment" section

- What workshops, training, information meetings and other dialogue sessions have been carried out to foster and grow your wanted culture and core values? It could be both planned and structured events as well as informal and unplanned sessions and events that have happened.
- What has been the purpose and objective of these activities? Who or how many have been involved and when did they take place?

For the "Follow up & Reflection" section

- What measurements have been done in the last period that could give us an understanding of our own and key stakeholders' perceptions of our culture?
- It could be attitude surveys, engagement surveys, Culture Values Assessment and other assessments that visualise our climate and satisfaction among our employees.
- It could be Customer Satisfaction Surveys or Supplier and Partner review meetings that have brought to the surface the satisfactions and perceptions of our behaviour and performance in the relationship and interface with our external stakeholders.
- It could also be outcomes and conclusions from regular meetings and reflection and learning sessions that have been carried out.

For the "Secure Consistency" section

- What are our wanted culture, values and/or norms of behaviour that we have defined and agreed that we would like to grow and develop?
- What are the behaviours and attitudes that we want to reach our long term strategic ambitions and short term plans?

5. Prepare a slide presentation (or a draft Culture Report) that could be used at your quarterly review meeting. Send out the material prior to your meeting so that everyone can come better prepared for the team to focus on reflections and conclusions.

DEFINE AND WRITE YOUR CULTURE REPORT

1. Before you start to work with the collected data, make sure you review the purpose and objectives of your Culture Report.
2. Appoint a note taker. It is suggested that you view what is said and concluded during this meeting either on a flipchart, whiteboard or a computer screen. This will make your dialogue and discussions more transparent and focused. Also, you can more easily capture the essence of your reflection and write it into your Culture Report at the end of your meeting.
3. Work step-by-step through the collected data starting with the "Create Dialogue" section.
4. Make sure that the data collected in all sections gives a correct and honest picture of your reality during the last period. Make adjustments if needed.
5. Look at the total picture and have a reflection (remember that the reflection should be based on dialogue and not discussion) by asking yourself:
   - What are you proud and happy about?
   - What can we learn, or what have we learned from our experience of this exercise?
   - What would we like to do differently in the coming period?
6. Pay special attention to the section "Follow up & Reflection" and ask yourself:
   - What becomes clear to you/us when we see the results of our different measurements?
   - Are there any patterns or themes that we can identify that will help us understand the dynamics of our culture better?
   - When looking on what we have done or not done in the "Create Dialogue" and the "Daily Alignment" section, are there any new insights or learning that we should add in our "Follow up & Reflection" section?
7. Pay special attention to the section "Secure Consistency" and ask yourself:
   - Is there anything that we need to reinforce, do differently or add, in order to better grow our wanted culture and core values?
8. Finalize your reflection by reading the collected statements and conclusions and come to agreement on what should or should not be in the official report.
9. Write your Culture Report. It should not be longer than two pages. See template example on the next pages.

COMMUNICATION OF CULTURE REPORT

1. Agree within your Management Team how and to whom you would like to communicate your Culture Report.
   The objective is to use the Culture Report to communicate our culture development to our Steering Committee or Board, and internally to all our employees.
2. It is recommended that the communication of the written report is supported by a short reflection involving and connecting the leaders and employees in your cultural development.
3. In time it may be valuable to review your progress over a longer time period, for example, a year. That could be done by reading the four last reports and then having a reflection session of what we can see and learn.

HANDOUT

CULTURE REPORT

The way we manage and develop our culture could be presented in four different phases. Each phase has its own focus and purpose, but with strong impact on each other. We present them as a continuous spinning wheel. This report is structured accordingly.

Create Dialogue: Develop new structures and approaches for active dialogues to reach our defined strategic focus areas.
Daily Alignment: Activities and focused dialogues ongoing, to promote our wanted cultural transformation.
Follow up & Reflection: What we measure and learn from our present culture and daily alignment activities.
Secure Consistency: Defined focus areas that need to be strengthened based on our follow up and reflections.

1. CREATE DIALOGUE

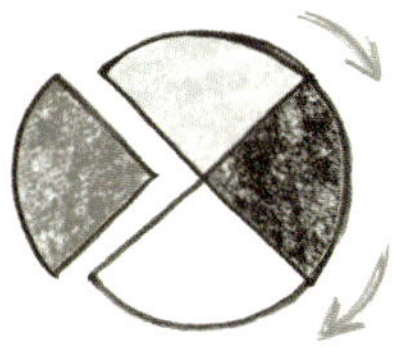

2. DAILY ALIGNMENT

HANDOUT

Culture Report

3. FOLLOW UP & REFLECTION

4. SECURE CONSISTENCY

CREATIVE MIND - MEDITATION

Session Leader Guide

Creative Mind is a meditation technique that offers the opportunity to expand your awareness. We encourage you to take the time to connect to your body, mind, spirit and soul. This meditation has the potential to help you induce the optimum level of consciousness for any given situation and experience the wisdom to create new possibilities.

PURPOSE

Through individual meditation, slow down our brainwaves in order to connect to our inner wisdom.

OBJECTIVE

Reach a better understanding, clarity and creativity, and to relax and heal our body, mind and spirit.

BEFORE STARTING

- Be clear on your intentions. If you invite others to do this meditation state clearly the purpose and objective. Some people may misinterpret the motivation for an invitation to meditate. The professional reasons to meditate are simply:
  - To slow down the brainwaves to connect better to your creative mind.
  - To slow down the brainwaves to help deal with a stressful situation.
  - Slowing down to heal your body, mind and spirit will improve your individual ability to deal with challenging and difficult situations.
- You can download the Creative Mind Meditation for free at www.valuescentre.com/getconnected in MP3 format.

PREPARATION FOR A MEDITATION

1. Find a place where you can be undisturbed for at least 25 minutes.
2. Sit down in a comfortable position with your hands resting on your knees.
3. Use a PC with speakers or headphones, or an mp3 player to play the meditation.
4. Listen and follow the instructions.

Tip: Bring pen and paper to write down what has become clear to you after the session.

HANDOUT

The introduction to the meditation will guide you to calm, heal and relax your, mind, body and spirit. It may help to familiarise yourself with some of the words used in the instructions. They are shown below.

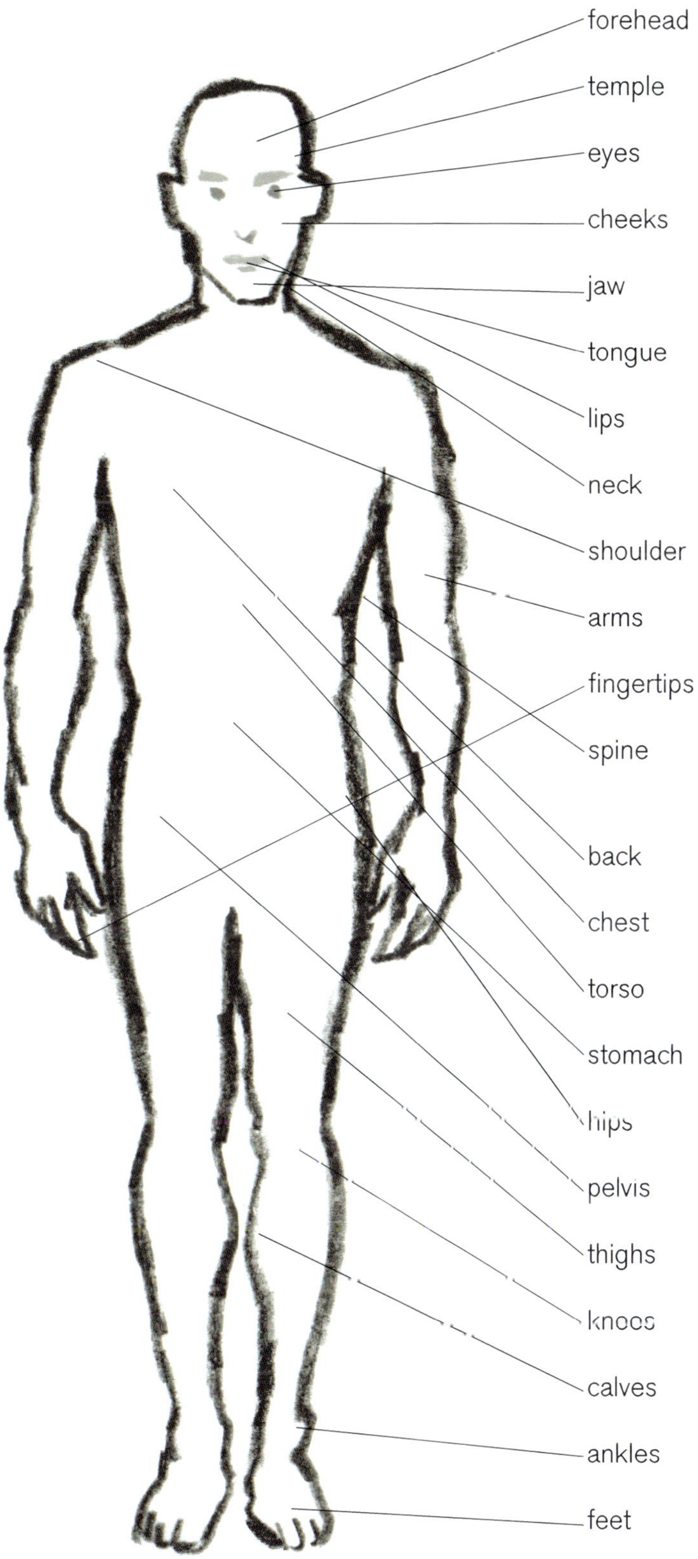

Why do the Creative Mind meditation?

Scientists have been measuring the electrical impulses the brain generates. These impulses are known as brainwaves.

Brainwaves, like all waves, are measured in two ways. The first is frequency, or speed of the electrical impulses. Frequency is measured in cycles per second (cps or Hz). The second measurement is amplitude, or the strength of the brainwave. Brainwaves range from 0.5 cps to 38 cps and are categorized into four frequencies: beta, alpha, theta, and delta. Each of these is explained below.

BETA brainwaves are the fastest frequencies ranging from 14 cycles per second up to 38 cycles per second. Beta is your normal thinking state, your active awareness and thought processes. Without beta you would not be able to function in the outside world.

ALPHA brainwaves are the brainwaves of relaxed detached awareness, visualization, sensory imagery and light reverie. They range between about 9 and 14 cycles per second. Alpha is the gateway to meditation and provides a bridge between the conscious and the subconscious mind.

THETA brainwaves are the subconscious mind. They range from about 4 to 8 cycles per second. Theta brainwaves occur during dreaming sleep and also during deep meditation. Theta also provides peak experiences such as creative inspiration or times of spiritual connection.

DELTA brainwaves are your subconscious mind, the sleep state, ranging from about 4 cycles per second down to 0.5 cycles per second. However, it may also be present in combination with other brainwaves in a waking state, acting as a form of radar, reaching out to understand at the deepest subconscious level things that we can't understand through thought processes. Delta is present in our experience of intuition, empathetic understanding and instinctual insight.

The **Creative Mind** is the term used to describe when the brainwave pattern combines all these characteristics of the different brainwave frequencies at the same time. This brainwave pattern can be found during "peak experience" and in all forms of creativity and high performance. It is a brainwave pattern shared by people in higher states of consciousness. It also appears at the instant of solving a problem, or getting an insight. The "ah-ha" experience.

It combines the intuitive, empathetic radar of the delta waves, the creative inspiration, personal insight, and spiritual awareness of the theta waves, the bridging capacity and relaxed, detached, awareness of the alpha waves, and the external attention and ability to consciously process thought of beta waves.

The **Creative Mind** technique focuses on the breath. You focus solely on the breath, both when you are breathing in and when you are breathing out. If you become aware of a thought, simply acknowledge the thought and return your focus to your breath. The incidence of thoughts will decrease and your inner expanded silence will have the potential to enhance wisdom, creativity and spiritual experience.

Scientific research indicates that a relaxed body is the first step to achieving a relaxed mind. A guide to physical relaxation is included on the Introduction to the meditation.

With regular practice, you will be able to relax almost instantly when preparing for meditation. Additionally, in time, you will be able to scan your body for tension and when you find it, focus on relaxing those specific muscle groups.

6
ADDITIONAL MATERIAL AND REFERENCES

Author	Title
Richard Barrett	Liberating the Corporate Soul Building a Values-Driven Organization The New Leadership Paradigm Love, Fear and the Destiny of Nations What My Soul Told Me The Values Driven Organisation
Ken Blanchard	Whale Done
Joseph Campbell	The Hero with a Thousand Faces
Centre for Creative Leadership	Ongoing Feedback: How to Get It, How to Use It – – An Ideas into Action Guidebook
Stephen M.R. Covey	Speed of Trust
Sue Annis Hammond, and Andrea B. Mayfield	The Thin Book of Naming Elephants: How to Surface Undiscussables for Greater Organizational Success
Laura Joffe Numeroff	If You Give a Mouse a Cookie
Dewitt Jones	DVD "Celebrate What's Right with the World"
David Kolb	Source of Learning & Development
Jim Kouzes and Barry Posner	The Leadership Challenge
James P. Lewis	Team-Based Project Management
St Lukes	Innovative Resources
Project Management Institute	Code of ethics and professional conduct
Carl Rogers	On becoming a person
Tony Schwartz, Catherine McCarthy	Manage Your Energy, Not Your Time
Peter Senge, Richard Ross, Bryan Smith, Art Kleiner, Charlotte Roberts	The Fifth Discipline Fieldbook
Dr Seuss	Lencioni: 5 dysfunctions of a team I can read with my eyes shut Horton hears a who
Will Shutz	FIRO: A Three-Dimensional Theory of Interpersonal Behavior
Rajendra S. Sisodia, David B. Wolfe and Jagdish N. Sheth	Firms of Endearment
Murray Stein	Transformation
Bruce Tuckman	Developmental sequence in small groups
Sloan R. Weitzel	Feedback That Works
John Whitmore	Coaching for Performance
Ken Wilber	A brief History of Everything

Web sites

Barrett Values Centre	www.valuescentre.com
The New Leadership Paradigm	http://tnlp.valuescentre.com

DIALOGUE TOOLS FOR WHOLE SYSTEM CHANGE

SEVEN LEVELS OF CONSCIOUSNESS©

Level	Personal	Organisational	Community/Society
7 Service	**Selfless service** Being your purpose. Compassion, humility, forgiveness. Caring for humanity and the planet	**Service to humanity and societal contribution** Social responsibility, long-term perspective, ethics, compassion and humility.	**Global sustainability** Human rights, long-term perspective, ecological resilience, peace, focus on future generations. Global perspective.
Making a difference	**Making a positive difference in the world** Living your purpose. Empathy, alliances, intuition, mentoring and focus on wellbeing (physical, emotional, mental, spiritual).	**Internal/External collaboration, community involvement** Environmental awareness, employee fulfilment, coaching/mentoring and caring for the local community.	**Strategic alliances and regional partnerships** Regional collaboration, environmental awareness, quality of life, community involvement and sustainability. Caring for nature.
Internal Cohesion	**Finding meaning in existence** Finding your purpose. Integrity, honesty, authenticity, passion, enthusiasm, creativity, and humour & fun.	**Sense of purpose and strong internal community** Shared vision and values. Commitment, creativity, enthusiasm, integrity, honesty, generosity, fairness, openness, transparency and trust.	**Strong cohesive culture** Shared vision and values. Fairness, transparency, trust, honesty and social cohesion. Positive collective spirit.
Transformation	**Letting go of fears** Finding the courage to grow and develop. Adaptability, life long learning, continuous renewal and personal growth.	**On-going improvement and employee participation** Adaptability, accountability, empowerment, teamwork, goals orientation and continuous improvement.	**Democratic processes and continuous renewal** Freedom, equality, empowerment, accountability, adaptability, entrepreneurship and consensus.
Self-esteem	**Feeling a sense of self-worth** Confidence, competence, self-reliance. Fear: *I am not enough.* Leads to need for power, authority or status seeking.	**High performance systems and processes** Reliability, quality, efficiency, productivity and excellence. Bureaucracy, hierarchy, confusion, and complacency.	**Institutional effectiveness** Law abiding, community/national pride, governmental efficiency and high quality public services. Bureaucracy, central control, elitism, complacency and apathy.
Relationship	**Feeling protected and loved** Family, friendship, loyalty, respect. Fear: *I am not loved enough.* Leads to jealousy, blame and discrimination.	**Positive relationships** that support organisation needs Loyalty, open communication, customer satisfaction. Manipulation, blame, favouritism and internal competition.	**Sense of belonging and social stability** Neighbourliness, conflict resolution, racial harmony and a focus on family and friendships. Inequality, discrimination, intolerance, hatred, loneliness/isolation.
1 Survival	**Satisfying physiological and survival needs** Health, security, financial stability. Fear: *I do not have enough.* Leads to control, domination and caution.	**Financial viability and people safety** Financial performance, organisational growth, and employee health and safety. Control, greed, exploitation and micro-management.	**Economic stability and citizen security** Prosperity, health care, employment, emergency services/defence and social safety nets. Corruption, violence, poverty, environmental pollution and greed.

Common Good

Self interest

Positive Focus/ Excessive Focus

Thank You!

We would like to express our deepest appreciation and thanks to Volvo IT for letting us use their experience and tools as a base for this book. We would especially like to thank Per Hellsten (Culture Navigator) and Sasha Hamilton (Project Manager) for their contribution in writing the first edition of this book.

We would also like to dedicate our heartiest thanks to all colleagues at Barrett Values Centre and the network of Cultural Transformation Tools (CTT) consultants who have supported us and given us good advice and feedback in the process of writing this book.

This book could never have been written without your feedback and the time we spent together in workshops and dialogues.

TOR ENEROTH

Network Director at Barrett Values Centre since 2010. Culture Manager at Volvo IT between 2000 - 2011. Between 1984 and 2000 he was manager and internal consultant for such areas as quality, change management, Leadership development and culture at Mölnlycke AB and SCA AB. Co-author of the book "The Dynamics of Change".
tor@valuescentre.com
www.valuescentre.com

NIRAN JIANG

Director at the Institute of Human Excellence. Previously a university professor and corporate executive, she has been a management advisor, facilitator and coach to aid personal and organisational transformation for the past 15 years.
niran@ihexcellence.org
www.ihexcellence.org

PLEUNTJE VAN MEER

Founded the Synnova network in 2002.
Operates globally as executive (team)coach and partner for businesses to implement whole systems change. She focuses on improving business impact by creating better connections, strengthening the culture and clarifying strategic alignment.
p.vanmeer@synnova.com
www.synnova.com

PHIL CLOTHIER

CEO at Barrett Values Centre since 2007. Opened the European operations for BVC in 2001 and until 2007 led the Cultural Transformation Tools global training program. Previous background in both social care and information communications technology.
phil@valuescentre.com
www.valuescentre.com

HÉCTOR INFER

Managing Partner at Transform Action Spain. Lead the development and deployment of Business Units in 16 countries of Latin America and Spain, working from HQ's in USA & UK, and Regional Centres of Brazil, Argentina and Mexico.
As an independent consultant, he has implemented Cultural Transformation Processes in organisations in Europe and Latin America since 1990.
hinfer@transform-action.net
www.transform-action.net

Everyone are certified trainers in Culture Transformation Tools (CTT). For more information go to www.valuescentre.com/trainings_events

* 1 3 5 2 7 4 3 8 1 *A